Restoring the Vision

*dedicated to the memory
of a lovely young lady, our daughter Debbie
a sensitive and caring nurse
who has already made the spiritual journey
from the kingdom on earth
to the kingdom in the glorious presence
of Jesus the king*

"Blessed are the pure in heart,
for they shall see God."
(Matthew 5:8)

Restoring the Vision

The Kingdom of God, the Church of the Future

Graham Tucker

Anglican Book Centre
Toronto, Canada

Published 1998 by

Anglican Book Centre
600 Jarvis Street
Toronto, Ontario
Canada M4Y 2J6

Copyright © Graham Tucker

All rights reserved. No part of this book may be reproduced, stored in a retrieval system, or transmitted, in any form or by any means, electronic, mechanical, photocopying, recording, or otherwise, without the written permission of the Anglican Book Centre Publishing.

This book has been published with the assistance of a grant from the College of Bishops of the Diocese of Toronto.

Unless otherwise specified, biblical quotations are from the *New International Version*. Grand Rapids: Zondervan, 1995.

Canadian Cataloguing in Publication Data
Tucker, Graham
    Restoring the vision: the kingdom of God, the church of the future

ISBN 1-55126-216-9

1. Kingdom of God. 2. Church Renewal. 3. Church and the world. I. Title.

BT94.T82 1998   231.7'2   C98-930262-8

Table of Contents

Introduction 7

Section A. Losing the Vision 11
Chapter 1. The Kingdom Vision 12
Chapter 2. From Kingdom to Church 24

Section B. Seeking the Vision 37
Chapter 3. Loving Relationship 38
Chapter 4. Responsible Stewardship 49

Section C. Finding the Vision 61
Chapter 5. From Church to Kingdom 62
Chapter 6. The Kingdom World 77

Epilogue 91
Parables of the Kingdom 93
Bibliography 94

Introduction

There are many indications that mainline churches in the Western world are in serious trouble. Church membership and attendance statistics for the major denominations in North America show a steady downward trend, beginning around 1970. Given the typical age profile of most congregations today, any extrapolation into the future is cause for alarm.

But life, death, and resurrection are basic to our Christian understanding of existence. Some things must decline and die before they can be restored to new life. This cycle applies to the church. Much that we know may have to pass away if the church is to rise to new life and vitality in the twenty-first century.

This prospect is both exciting and challenging. Loren Mead of the Alban Institute in Washington notes that

> we are at the front edges of the greatest transformation of the church that has occurred for 1,600 years.... That transformation is occurring because of the persistent call of God that our whole world be made new, and that the church's mission in that world be itself transformed in new patterns of reconciling the world to God" (*The Once and Future Church*, p. 68).

Both Loren Mead in the United States and Reginald Bibby in Canada have extensively analyzed the problems of the modern church. Their research has confirmed my own observations.

In the late 1970s, I helped to found the King-Bay Chaplaincy, a ministry to the downtown Toronto business community. My work in the corporate world convinced me that both local congregations and regional church structures have much to learn from modern techniques of management and organizational development. But I have no illusions that improved efficiency and revised structure can save the church. For many years, I served as director of the Aurora Conference Centre, a facility for clergy and lay training in the Anglican Diocese of Toronto. I worked with many congregations on various approaches to renewal, all of which seemed to make a significant difference, but they did not solve the problem. Although the decline in membership decreased, it also continued.

Clearly, the problem is much too deep to be remedied by improved ways of carrying on the traditional life and practice of the church.

In our time, there has been a profound shift in human awareness. The sight of earth from the moon has forever changed our world view. One of the most significant changes began when, as Marshall McLuhan observed, the communications revolution turned the world into a "global village." TV satellites now enable us to see whatever is newsworthy as it happens, anywhere on the planet. The world's stock exchanges provide us with instant indicators of global economic change. National boundaries mean little to powerful multinational corporations, and common markets make economic isolation increasingly difficult. The human race is being forced by information technology to learn to live in what we hope will eventually be an interdependent cooperative world community.

With the growth of an integrated global economy has come a renewed realization of the holistic human economy. The popular movement toward alternative medicine regards true health as involving the whole person — body, mind, and spirit. Similarly, enlightened business organizations are discovering a spiritual component in human relations, ethics, and the environment. But the church's teaching and practice seem conspicuously to lag behind the new consciousness; they are couched in old thought forms that separate the spiritual from the material, the sacred from the secular, and lead to misunderstandings and conflicts. Such compartmentalizing of life makes it possible for some people to say prayers in church and allow violence in their communities. It is no wonder that many thinking people, particularly of the younger generation, dismiss religion as irrelevant at best and dangerous at worst.

Our experience of the global village is forcing us to face the reality of an interdependent world community, in which we must come to terms with cultural, racial, and religious diversity. In the light of this reality, the exclusive and often conflicting claims of traditional mainline denominations, and the plethora of peripheral religious sects, make it difficult for people not brought up in those traditions to take seriously the Christian vision of "one Lord, one faith, one baptism; one God and Father of all" (Ephesians 4:5–6).

For the past 1,600 years, the church has often functioned on imperialistic assumptions that have sanctioned the use of power to dominate life rather than serve it. Such behaviour is now recognized as a distorted expression of Christianity, which actually inverts many of the values taught by Jesus. Most Christian traditions have been not only indifferent but hostile to nature, seeing it as devoid of spiritual value, or even as a source of corruption. Under the pressure of the emerging holistic consciousness, the Christian era, known as Christendom, is now coming to an end. Many people today are seeking a spirituality that embraces the natural order and recognizes the growing ecological crisis.

In our time, people are discovering the one branch of the Christian church that did not conform to the assumptions and practices of Christendom but developed in a different context not controlled by Rome. This was the Celtic church, which flourished in Ireland and Britain between the fifth and seventh centuries, while the rest of Europe was entering a dark age of conflict and division after the fall of the Roman Empire.

Under the leadership of St. Columba of Iona and St. Ninian of Lindisfarne and their monks, Scotland and Northern England and parts of Europe were converted to a Celtic Christianity that focused primarily on the vision of the kingdom of God. We cannot turn back the clock, but we can learn from the Celts. It is their vision of the kingdom life taught by Jesus that I am advocating as the way to transform the church for the future.

Fifty years ago Sir George MacLeod of the Church of Scotland had the vision of rebuilding the ancient abbey on the island of Iona, as a practical symbol for rebuilding the church. Now, toward the end of my ministry, the Spirit has led me to explore what it was about my own experience of Iona that so powerfully influenced my life. The purpose of this book is to consider how the church has largely lost Jesus' vision of the kingdom of God on earth, and how we can recover that vision and build on it.

How to Use This Book

This book is designed for individual reading and reflection. But because it focuses on living the Christian life, it will be most helpful as a resource for small-group work.

Groups of eight to ten people are most effective for this type of study, reflection, and action. Meetings can begin with worship (including prayer, a scripture reading related to the theme of a chapter to be studied, and silence for reflection), followed by guided study of the chapter. The chapters lend themselves to six group-sessions of about one-and-a-half hours. The study and reflection may lead to decisions about more intentional "kingdom" lifestyles, parish worship, and action in the world. The introduction can be read by group members in preparation for the first meeting, which may be spent in building the group and sharing ideas and questions about the kingdom of God. Participants can read the following chapter in advance of the next group meeting.

Section A
Losing the Vision

Chapter 1
The Kingdom Vision

> The church, when it lost the vision that the kingdom was coming, also lost the theology that enabled it to live as though the kingdom was at hand (Constance Parvey).

The Power of Jesus' Message

It was a stressful time, not unlike our own. Life was hard for many in the Holy Land. Roman military occupation and religious oppression left them feeling helpless and afraid. People longed for a saviour who could free them from persecution and injustice. Into that time of tension and fear came a new kind of leader with a new kind of message.

One by one they heard the call and left everything to follow him. Some left successful fishing careers, one relinquished a lucrative tax collecting business, another gave up a revolutionary religious sect. The disciples represented all sorts and conditions of people, but they left everything to follow Jesus. And they were only the first! Soon throngs of people were seeking him and listening to him and hanging on his every word. "News about him spread all over Syria.... Large crowds from Galilee, the Decapolis, Jerusalem, Judea and the region across the Jordan followed him" (Matthew 4:24–25). He taught them, he healed them, and they were inspired and amazed.

Very quickly, Jesus' following took on the dimensions of a new religious movement. The gospels paint vivid pictures of the swelling crowds: "The number of those who ate was about five thousand men, besides women and children" (Matthew 14:13, 21). Not only was he attracting huge crowds, but his teaching was having a marked impact on society: "When Jesus entered Jerusalem, the whole city was stirred" (Matthew 21:9–10). Within three short years, he had attracted such attention that the political and religious rulers feared that civil order was endangered and their authority threatened. Why? What was the attraction?

The secret of Jesus' power to attract lay in the power of his message. He proclaimed, "The time has come. The kingdom of God is near. Repent and believe the good news!" (Mark 1:15). The gospel of the kingdom, and all that it promised for the future of the human race, was the compelling attraction. In the face of widespread injustice, cruelty, and oppression, Jesus taught the good news that God is on the side of the poor, the suffering, and the oppressed — that God is a God of love and compassion, willing to forgive sin and affirm the solidarity of the human race.

This was the appeal of Jesus of Nazareth, who not only preached the kingdom of God but lived by its radically different values. In his life and teaching, he embodied the kingdom for all to see, and those who were open to accepting his message were prepared to leave everything and follow him. He proclaimed a system of values, and demonstrated a style of leadership, that challenged the traditional concepts of human governance and citizenship, and initiated the reign of the kingdom of God.

A Transforming Vision

I believe that the rediscovery and application of the vision of the kingdom of God as lived and taught by Jesus has the power, in our time, to transform our suffering and despairing world into a "new world" of justice and peace. This was the central theme of the one prayer Jesus asked his followers to pray — that God's kingdom would come on earth as it is in heaven. This is the true calling and mission of the church in our time.

But what is the kingdom of God? How can we identify its salient features? In his life and teaching, Jesus gave us a clear picture of the values of the kingdom. Although he would rule as a king in the hearts of humanity, he chose to be born of poor parents in humble circumstances. His ministry was ordained by God, yet he sought accreditation by a popular local prophet. He refused the temptation to use divine power to attract a following and assert his authority. He directed his message to the common people and selected his followers from them, and they heard him gladly. In all things, he sought to do God's will.

He had compassion on the sick, the blind, and the lame, and healed them, in spite of the errors of their past. Recognizing personal needs before outdated customs, he healed and fed people on the Sabbath day, against the law. Although he risked damaging his own reputation, he associated freely with the despised and destitute. He criticized the ruling elites for being politically correct and preserving their own positions, rather than keeping justice and pursuing the common good. He submitted himself to humiliation and torture, and finally gave up his life for his friends. And when his followers were desolate and in despair, he came among them in Spirit to comfort and to guide them.

In his many sayings and parables, Jesus taught that loving relationships are primary in the kingdom. We must be as concerned about the welfare of others as about our own welfare (Matthew 22:37). The kingdom of God is within us (Luke 17:21). The care and protection of children is a sacred trust (Matthew 18:3). In spite of personal risk, the ideal citizen assists the wounded and marginalized in society (Luke 10:29). Instead of seeking retribution and revenge, we must minister to our enemies (Matthew 5:43). Although we have been offended and hurt repeatedly, there must be no end to our ability to forgive (Matthew 6:14). The greatest in the kingdom are those who serve others (Matthew 20:25). For in the kingdom, those who humble themselves shall be exalted (Luke 14:11).

A mark of a citizen in the kingdom is responsible stewardship or management of the resources given by God — both our lives and our planet. Because we are heirs, sons and daughters of God, we have a duty to use our inheritance wisely and to honour its source (John 15:15). We must be good custodians of what we have received (Matthew 25:29). Since much has been given to us, much will also be expected from us (Luke 12:48). Good stewards are trustworthy and accountable to the owner, managing the property wisely and distributing compensation fairly (Luke 12:42).

The message of the kingdom of God is particularly relevant to us today, because it was proclaimed in a time remarkably like our own. Jesus had the foresight to see that, unless Israel abandoned its quest for temporal power, it would be dispersed by the armies of Rome. People were afraid of the future. They sensed catastrophe ahead. With prophetic insight, Jesus read the signs of the times and said, "On the earth, nations will be in anguish and perplexity at the roaring and tossing of the sea. People will faint from terror, apprehensive of what is coming on the world" (Luke 21:25–26).

The Vision Lost

Within a few hundred years, the brave vision of the early church had succumbed to the forces of history. The church that Jesus had established as the instrument of God's reign on earth gradually lost sight of the kingdom as a present goal and recast it as a divine rescue at the end of time. The church ceased to be a "means" to the kingdom and became an "end" in itself. The story of Christendom, beginning with the conversion to Christianity of the Roman emperor Constantine in AD 312, is the sad story of struggles, divisions, and conflict within the church, a power-based approach to mission and ministry that was the antithesis of Jesus' teaching about the kingdom way.

To envision the kingdom today, we need to exercise discernment — a gift of the Spirit — and to draw near to Jesus the king. When a vision resonates with the human heart and the image of God in which we were created, it begins to come alive, and God's vision becomes our vision. When members of an organization or community, at any level, discover a higher purpose that has real meaning for them, everything changes.

Herein lies the potential for discovering the underlying unity of the human race from the perspective of the love, compassion, and grace of God.

To have lasting power, a shared vision must be related to a sense of vocation or calling. The Bible clearly indicates that the kingdom of God is destined to be the fulfillment of God's purpose for creation when "the kingdom of the world has become the kingdom of our Lord and of his Christ" (Revelation 11:15). We all have a part to play in furthering the kingdom on earth, but the burden of its fulfillment is in God's hands. If we see our individual and corporate commitment to the kingdom as a fulfillment of God's purpose, it gives a higher meaning to our life and work than any earthly vision could possibly give.

I believe that the present decline of the Western church is largely due to the loss of this vision of the kingdom. Also, many people accept that the long era of Christendom is now over. Together, these two perceptions present us with both the necessity and the opportunity to rediscover the heart of Jesus' message, and to recall his purpose. The kingdom of God provides us with a vision of renewal sufficiently expansive to unite all Christian churches in a common mission of world transformation in the power of the Spirit. The future of the church depends on restoring Jesus' teaching of the kingdom of God as the central ministry of our time.

Our Troubled Times

Any extrapolation of trends in the world today can lead us to frightening prospects. We are aware of problems that threaten the human race — population explosion, environmental pollution, unstable climatic conditions, natural resource depletion, continuing arms build-up fuelled by racial violence and worldwide terrorism. Together, these problems point to a fearful future. Our deepest concern is that no one seems to be in real control. The political and economic systems we have created, based on time-honoured assumptions and values, are not working for the majority of the human race or for the planet.

Hundreds of millions of people in the developing world are born to experience little more than pangs of hunger and pains of death. Malnutrition and disease are rampant. In developed nations, the gap between rich and poor is widening to disturbing dimensions, creating gross inequalities and threatening to destabilize the fabric of society. Our economic systems produce more and more wealth, but they seem incapable of ensuring that even the bare necessities of life are evenly distributed.

All over the planet, the natural environment is being raped and pillaged. Forests are burned for agriculture or cleared for lumber, watersheds are drained for new housing developments, rivers and lakes have become fetid sewers or chemical stews, the atmosphere is heavy with carbon dioxide and light on ozone, the earth is choked with urban rubbish and radioactive waste. Both the human economy and the global ecology are precariously out of balance. We do not know how much more abuse the planetary system can take before the scales may tip.

In recent history, we have seen some so-called Christian countries perpetrate ethnic murder and ecological savagery. Clearly, the false gods of nationalism and economic domination have overshadowed any influence that the church might have had. With a few notable exceptions, the modern church has moved into a defensive or survival mode and the reign of God is not proclaimed. Albert Nolan points out that

> organized religion has been very little help in this crisis. In fact, religion has sometimes tended to make matters worse. The type of religion that emphasizes a supernatural world *in such a way* that one does not need to be concerned about the future of this world and all its peoples, offers a form of escape that makes it all the more difficult to solve our problems *(Jesus Before Christianity*, p. 11).

The stakes are high and the task is urgent. In a world that seems to have no discernible meaning or purpose, anything goes. We act like a ship that has lost its bearings in a storm. We need a compass to help us find our spiritual "true north," to get our bearings, and to plot a course for the human journey.

Current Threats to Civilization

Before we can plot a new direction, we need to clarify our present position. We must first identify some of the forces at work in our society that are pushing us off course. One of the best summaries I have found of the destructive trends now threatening Western civilization was expressed by Charles Colson, founder of the Prison Fellowship, in his address entitled "The Enduring Revolution," given at the University of Chicago in 1993, when he received the million-dollar Templeton Prize for Progress in Religion.

A. The Relativity of Moral Values

One of the current "myths" of our time, according to Colson, is "the relativity of moral values."

> This myth dismisses the importance of family, church, and community; denies the value of sacrifice; and elevates individual rights and pleasures as the ultimate social value. But with no higher principles to live by, men and women suffocate under their own expanding pleasures. Consumerism becomes empty and levelling, leaving society full of possessions but drained of ideals *(The Enduring Revolution,* p. 7).

The psychological impact of our relativistic and materialistic value system was documented by Susan Crause Whitbourne, a professor of psychology at the University of Massachusetts, who found that since the 1960s, when she began a study of attitudes in America, there has been a loss of personal meaning. People are working harder but feeling greater despair. In her most recent testing, she found a "precipitous decline" in ego integrity, a personality factor relating to wholeness, honesty, and meaning in life, and to having a sense of connection with others. She concluded that there is a "general society-wide crisis of morality and purpose affecting adults of all ages" *(Psychology Today,* Jan./Feb. 1993).

B. Radical Individualism

Another modern "myth" identified by Colson is "radical individualism."

> This myth hides the dividing line between good and evil, noble and base. It has created a crisis in the realm of truth. When a society abandons its transcendent values, each individual's moral vision becomes purely personal and finally equal. Society becomes merely the sum total of individual preferences, and since no preference is morally preferable, anything that can be dared will be permitted *(The Enduring Revolution*, p. 6).

Colson finally points to the saving alternative facing the human race — the way of the kingdom of God.

> Our only decision is to welcome His rule or to fear it. But this gives everyone hope. For this is a vision beyond a vain utopia or a timid new world order. It is the vision of an Enduring Revolution *(The Enduring Revolution*, p. 16).

The Challenge for Today

The fundamental challenge facing those who share the vision of the kingdom of God is to counter the forces threatening to dehumanize our lives. How can we even approach this daunting task? We can learn to recognize the kingdom within ourselves and others. We can begin to practise the values of love and stewardship that Jesus taught (these two core values of the kingdom will be examined in Chapters 3 and 4). We can imagine small groups of faithful people, worshipping together in the name of Christ and discovering new fulfillment and effectiveness. We can envision business and professional people, working to promote ethics in the workplace and making a significant and enduring difference (small-group ministry and business ethics will be explored in Chapters 5 and 6). Jesus' vision of the kingdom provides a clear pattern and purpose for us. We have only to make that vision our own.

If the vision of the kingdom is to flourish on earth, we need a new style of leadership that reflects kingdom values. Stephen Covey says that leadership is "the ongoing process of keeping your vision and values before you and aligning your life to be congruent with those most important things" *(The Seven Habits of Highly Effective People,* p. 132*)*. In his life and work, Jesus modeled the concept of servant leadership. Although he was aware of his infinite power, he chose to wash his disciples' feet. It is a strange paradox that greatness comes from humility. A style of leadership that empowers others gains the kind of allegiance that millions have given to Christ throughout history. The power of the kingdom is service.

Nelson Mandela epitomizes this kind of leadership. For nearly thirty years Mandela was literally entombed in jail, yet he symbolized hope for the black people he represented. Nothing is more powerful than such symbols of hope; they get below the rational mind and touch the heart. I shall never forget watching on TV this tall dignified figure emerging from his jail tomb, waving to the crowds — the young radical lawyer transformed into an elder statesman for peace and reconciliation, ready to lead his people back to freedom. His release had strong biblical overtones, reminiscent of the one who came "to proclaim release for prisoners and recovery of sight to the blind, to let the broken victims go free." It was a rare moment of kingdom reality and servant leadership.

The Christian vision of the kingdom — a society of peace and joy, justice and human fulfilment — cannot but have universal appeal. We are called to live by the values of the kingdom of God, and to recognize that many of these values challenge the "means is the end" culture, currently overshadowing the world community. The kingdom of God provides a practical vision for people committed to making a difference. Verna Dozier has aptly expressed it.

> The people of God are called to help change the world.
> To help come into being a world in which every human

being knows that he or she is loved and valued. A world in which every human being knows that he or she has a contribution to make. A world in which every human being shares in some of the resources of creation *(Authority of the Laity)*.

Those who become members and inheritors of the kingdom of God are called to live with the true purpose of life in mind, to hope and work for a time when justice will be done and "the kingdom of the world has become the kingdom of our Lord and of his Christ, and he will reign for ever and ever" (Revelation 11:15).

A Personal Story

One fall evening, a small group of men talked about vocation — what did we feel called to be and to do in this world? As a coleader of the group, I was not expecting the question to be asked of me! To my surprise, my partner said, "And you, Brian, what are you being called to do at this moment in your life?" I am still struck by what happened next.

A very clear memory of the story of God's call to Abraham, to leave his home and go into a foreign country, leaped into my mind. At that moment, I became aware of being called to undertake a new ministry outside the comfortable place in the church where I was. I felt called to work in the "foreign territory" of industry and commerce where I still am today, some twelve years later — singing God's song in a new land!

A Meditation

Leave everything and follow you? How could I? My mortgage, my job, the new promotion that's coming. My house, the family, my community. You must be calling someone else.

The disciples were poor. They had little to leave, to follow you. It was easier in those days. Life was simple then. Yet I suppose they had families and homes, and jobs and communities. But did they have mortgages?

How does one leave everything and follow, yet be responsible to one's obligations at the same time? Jesus, how do we follow you in the real world? What is it that we should leave? Is it our goods and possessions? Or is it our attachment and love of these?

How do we centre our life on you in a complex and turbulent world? Perhaps make you the core of our desires and ambitions. Perhaps find some balance that we can live with. It is a struggle, Lord.

You call us to leave everything and follow you. Could the struggle be the first step? Help us take the second!

Brian Murray

For Individual Reflection or Group Discussion — Chapter 1

1. What was it about the life and teaching of Jesus that attracted the crowds? What was the basis of Jesus' power and ministry? Why did the religious and political leaders see Jesus as a threat?

2. What do you think would be the essence of Jesus' message to the church today? (Reflect on Mark 1:14–20 and Matthew 21:28–32.)

3. If the decline of the church is caused by something much deeper than the need for improved ways of carrying on the traditional life and practice of the church, what could be the true cause or causes?

4. What are some of the forces in our society that are most resistant to the Christian message in our time? What are some of the implications of the similarity between Jesus' time and our own time?

5. To what extent and in what ways has the church become an end in itself? What are the implications of this for the advancement of the kingdom?

6. To what extent is the Christian faith a matter of personal relationship with God? What difference would it make to your Christian commitment if you believed that Jesus' teaching provides a value framework and action plan for all of life, including the workplace and society?

7. (The group leader could bring several newspapers from the previous week and invite group members to take a few minutes, in pairs, to identify stories that challenge a Christian perspective, and to reflect on the "myths" described by Charles Colson.) Do you think that Jesus' vision of the kingdom has the power to counter the forces that threaten to dehumanize our lives?

Chapter 2

From Kingdom to Church

> If anyone is in Christ, he is a new creation;
> the old has gone, the new has come!
> (2 Corinthians 5:17).

In the first few years of the early church, the teaching of the apostles brought a different emphasis to Jesus' teaching, so that gradually the church became more concerned about what people believed than how they acted. And within a few hundred years, the church hierarchy sought strong alliances with secular power, in order to protect its position and extend its sway. As a result, the vision of the kingdom was diverted to the establishment of an institution. How did this come about?

A New Spiritual Paradigm

Seeing the kingdom as a present reality with world-changing potential requires a paradigm shift, both for the church and the world. A paradigm is the way we interpret reality. It is our "world view," our understanding of the nature of things and how they work. The scientific world was forced to make a radical paradigm shift when Galileo, with his newly-made telescope, proved that the earth circled the sun. Before, everyone had thought that the earth was the centre of the universe.

It usually takes a long time to work out the implications of a major paradigm shift. We naturally resist having to change deeply held assumptions, attitudes, and beliefs. Jesus and his message of the kingdom was just such a paradigm shift. His teaching departed so radically from the ideas of his time — and so threatened the status quo — that the state and religious leaders arranged his death.

Jesus came not only to proclaim the advent of the kingdom of God. He deliberately set out to redefine the whole meaning of kingship. He presented a radically different image of authority from that held by most people of his time, and even today. Until the church comes to terms with Jesus' model of the kingdom, it will continue largely as it has throughout history, trying to function by worldly power and control, rather than through sacrificial love and humility, which is at the heart of the kingdom of God.

A King and a Servant

Jesus was a very unorthodox king. He possessed none of the traditional trappings of worldly power. Instead, he exercised the incredible strength of divine love. He was a personal charismatic leader with a deep understanding of human nature. "He did not need man's testimony about man, for he knew what was in a man" (John 2:25). And those who meet him today know that he sees right through them to the core of their being, yet with the transforming power of his healing love.

Instead of turning the religious hierarchy upside down or establishing a new one, Jesus questioned the very need for hierarchy. The kingdom is a "flat organization." It has taken the business community a long time to discover the merits of bottom-up management. In God's kingdom, the values of service and compassion replace those of dominance and control. Everyone is the greatest! There are no second-class citizens. "Whoever practises and teaches these commands will be called great in the kingdom of heaven" (Matthew 5:19).

Kingdom people love God and others as much as themselves, and humility overcomes pride. "Everyone who exalts himself will be humbled, and he who humbles himself will be exalted" (Luke 14:11). Jesus also said, "You know that the rulers of the

Gentiles lord it over them, and their high officials exercise authority over them. Not so with you. Instead, whoever wants to become great among you must be your servant, and whoever wants to be first must be your slave — just as the Son of Man did not come to be served, but to serve, and to give his life as a ransom for many" (Matthew 20:25–28).

At the end of Jesus' earthly ministry, the chief priest sent him to Pilate, the Roman governor, who had the authority to put him to death. In the course of the interrogation, Pilate asked Jesus if he was a king. Jesus replied, "My kingdom is not of this world. I'm not that kind of king, not the world's kind of king" (*The Message*, John 18:36). Jesus meant not that the values of his kingdom were other worldly, but that they challenged the values of this world. He is a different kind of king, indeed! His crown was a circle of thorns, and his throne was a wooden cross! But because there is no greater love than giving for others, his real throne is the human heart. When Christ reigns in the heart, our entire world view changes. We adopt a new paradigm.

The Shift from Kingdom to Church

It is inevitable that any dedicated and purposeful human community will eventually become institutionalized. This is true of a business, a political movement, a religion. It is neither good nor bad. Large organizations are often necessary to protect and advance the interests of their members in a larger society. But impersonal organizations can often be seduced into self-preservation and aggrandizement at the expense of their members. Institutions tend to corrupt those at the seat of power, and corruption in religious institutions can spawn cruelty and evil. In the church, the quest for power and control led eventually to a departure from the values of the kingdom of God.

The process by which Christianity grew from a Jewish sect centred in Jerusalem to a powerful church centred in Rome is documented in the New Testament. It is here that confusion about Jesus' teaching on the kingdom becomes apparent. If we trace the roots of the early Christian community, we will see how the church grew away from the vision taught by Jesus. Although there are points of contact, the church and the kingdom are not the same.

The story began at least 2,000 years before Jesus' time, when God called Abraham to be the father of a chosen people who would hold a special covenant relationship with God. In the scriptures of the Old Testament, we read of the long and troubled saga of the Jewish nation in their struggle to maintain the covenant. Jesus understood his mission to be in the tradition of God's relationship with the Hebrew people. In his short three-year ministry of preaching, teaching, and healing, he sought to clarify God's purpose and establish God's kingdom. From among his followers, he chose the twelve apostles to initiate and lead the Christian community. This community was called to live by Jesus' values and to teach the way of the kingdom on earth as it is in heaven.

But it did not take long for the focus to shift from the kingdom to the church. Although Jesus speaks about the kingdom over a hundred times in the gospels, he mentions the church only twice (Matthew 16:18 and 18:17). These references are probably later interpolations, because the church was not organized until after the death and resurrection of Jesus. In those portions of the New Testament written after the resurrection, the kingdom is mentioned only thirty-two times, including a mere thirteen times in Paul's letters. In fact, Paul's writings seldom refer directly to Jesus' life or teaching. Although the kingdom is clearly no longer the central theme, the church is mentioned over a hundred times in the post-resurrection period. This marks a profound shift in emphasis!

The Christian community, which Jesus intended to be an instrument for the extension of his kingdom on earth, became the church. And over the years, the church became institutionalized as an end in itself.

The Secular Power of the Church

As the church grew, it not only altered the emphasis of Jesus' teaching, but actually abandoned the kingdom paradigm. To advance its own interests, the church sought alliance with the state and, adopting structures of authority and control, turned away from the kingdom of justice, love, and service taught by Jesus. By the third century after the founding of Christianity, the church had developed from a minority movement into a powerful institution. It had acquired an organizational structure, property and buildings, and political power and influence.

In his book *The Steward*, Douglas Hall describes the transformation of servant Christianity into an imperialistic form of Christendom. In AD 312, after the conversion of the Emperor Constantine, the Roman Empire was "baptized" into a nominal Christianity. In the fight to control Italy, the armies of Constantine I met those of Maxentius. Before the battle, Constantine, who was already sympathetic to Christianity, claimed to have seen in the sky a flaming cross inscribed with the words, "in this sign thou shalt conquer." He adopted the symbol of the cross and was victorious. This battle is regarded as a turning point for Christianity. In 313 Constantine issued the Edict of Milan, which stated that Christianity would be tolerated throughout the empire. Before this, the followers of Jesus had been a powerless, outlawed, and persecuted sect.

Constantine continued to tolerate paganism while he endeavoured to unify and strengthen Christianity. He was responsible for initiating the first great church councils, beginning with the Council of Nicea in 325, which promulgated the Nicene Creed, a foundation document for the doctrines of the church. As the founder of the Christian Empire, Constantine began a new era that transformed the church. Under his rule, membership in the church become comparatively easy and encouraged a nominal kind of Christianity that required little knowledge of the teachings and values of Jesus.

The church as institution increasingly allied itself with political power, and the bishops — particularly the bishop of Rome — functioned as princes of the church, in close cooperation with secular rulers. In AD 800, when Pope Leo III crowned Charlemagne as emperor, the church became deeply involved with the interests of the Holy Roman Empire. In 1232, at the insistence of secular powers, Pope Gregory IX commissioned the mendicant orders (mainly Dominican and Franciscan monks) to investigate charges of heresy. The church subsequently established the notorious inquisition, which used fear and torture to force people to recant "errors of doctrine" and accept the "true faith."

At the same time that the institution of the church was becoming more deeply embroiled in the machinations of secular power, individual Christians were responding to Jesus' message with faithful and sometimes dangerous commitment. From the earliest days of the Christian faith, those who championed their beliefs in the face of cruel authority often met with captivity, torture, and death — even from the church itself. Many devout people made long pilgrimages to holy places, as a discipline of penance or devotion. During the fourth century in Europe, people desiring to lead holy lives away from the demands of the world formed monastic communities, took vows of poverty, chastity, and obedience, and gave themselves to prayer and homely labour.

Even the ecclesiastical corridors of power were inhabited by good and faithful people. St. Gregory the Great, pope between 590 and 604, was a holy and devout man. He built monasteries, directed vast sums of money to charity, and wrote a number of devotional works. But he was also a consummate negotiator and administrator. He brought peace from warring invaders and firmly established the temporal power of the papacy. And so, in spite of the faithfulness of countless individual Christians, the administrative structures of the church continued to accumulate wealth and authority. Even some monasteries grew rich and proud. Over the centuries, Jesus' vision of a kingdom promoting love and service gave way to an institution wielding power and control.

Now at the end of the twentieth century, with the increasing secularization of society, the Constantinian paradigm of a powerful church (the myth of Christendom) is crumbling. There is an urgent need to rethink the role of the church in our society. In the guise of a crisis, we have been given an opportunity! It is vital for the future of Christianity that the reconstruction of the church, so desperately needed today, take place in accordance with Jesus' vision of the kingdom. If we cannot always find Christ in the institution, we must look for him in the community, where people meet together in his name.

The Church in Today's World

For many people the church is about sitting in a pew. It's about hymns and choirs and clergy and sermons, about liturgies and committees and parish groups, about offering envelopes and building maintenance. But it's also about being with others and speaking with God, about working and worshipping together. A recent pamphlet, entitled *Churching the Unchurched* by John Throop, suggests ways to help people feel comfortable in the strange culture of the church. But it raises an obvious question: "Is all of this church custom and culture what Jesus was asking his followers to do in obedience to his teaching?"

Robert Raines tells a story about an English bishop who once said, "Everywhere Paul went there was a revolution, but everywhere I go they serve tea." Christians are called to turn the world upside down, but too often they feel like the bishop — certainly comfortable, but maybe ineffectual.

Our first task is to get a distinct picture of what we are asking when we pray, "thy kingdom come," so that we can be more intentional about living the kingdom lifestyle today. A clear focus on the kingdom is likely to make us anything but "comfortable" in the church. To understand what Jesus meant when he declared that the kingdom of God was at hand, and that we should always pray that it would come on earth, is to hold the key to the Christian message. Such understanding integrates, and gives meaning and purpose, to the whole biblical revelation.

First of all, the kingdom that Jesus taught is about *loving relationship:*

- our relationship to God and creation;
- our relationship to the people around us — family, friends, coworkers;
- our relationship to the people of the world — nations, races, religions.

Second, living in the kingdom is about *responsible stewardship:*

- our responsibility to the world of work, productivity, creativity;
- our responsibility to the political system and human freedom;
- our responsibility to the natural environment and planetary ecology.

Living in the kingdom is about establishing a loving relationship with all humanity and restoring responsible stewardship toward God's creation. In so far as the church community focuses on these values, it becomes an instrument of the kingdom and advances the will of God.

We live in a world filled with fear and violence. Many people despair the lack of meaning in life. But the message of the kingdom truly brings good news. In the kingdom of God, there is purpose to existence. Jesus taught a value system that could transform human relationships in the global village, he taught a stewardship perspective that would enable all people to live in peace and plenty on this planet. The kingdom message provides the possibility of a new paradigm, a new world order worth living and working for. Surely this is good news that the world is dying to hear.

Once we have acknowledged Jesus, the servant-king, as our leader in the kingdom, and have followed his example of love and service, we will find that we have already passed from death to life. Our experience may then enable us to make sense of our existence and have hope for the future. The values of the kingdom will enable us to enjoy fullness of life on earth, and we shall discover what Jesus meant when he said, "I have come that they may have life, and have it to the full" (John 10:10). Now that's good news!

Evangelism and the Kingdom

Toward the end of his earthly ministry, Jesus told the parable of the sheep and the goats (Matthew 25:31–46). When he returns in glory, Jesus will separate those who are to be members of his kingdom from those who are to be cast out. But orthodoxy of belief will not be his standard of selection! The blessed ones will be those who are compassionate stewards, serving the needy and fighting for justice.

This parable presents two different perspectives on the gospel. On the one hand is Jesus the servant king, with a vital concern for human life and values in the world here and now. On the other hand is Jesus the saviour, who by his death and resurrection has opened for us the gate of heaven. I would argue that the shift in emphasis from servant to saviour has produced a lack of balance in the Christian message down through the ages, and that this distortion has contributed to the present weakness of the church. As a result, we have largely lost the vision of the kingdom and its power to transform life in the present moment.

It was partly the theology of St. Paul, so energetically expounded in his letters, that turned the emphasis away from Jesus' teaching of the kingdom. St. Paul's background and experience shaped his theology. His conversion from a strict Pharisee to a committed follower of Jesus was dramatic and powerful, but his Christian teaching remained persistently legalistic. According to Paul, believing in the power of Jesus' death and resurrection restored the relationship between the just God and a "sinner." Paul reasoned that we "are justified freely by his grace through the redemption that came by Christ Jesus. God presented him as a sacrifice of atonement, through faith in his blood" (Romans 3:24).

The good news of the gospel includes two main elements. One is a reasoned proposition after the teaching of Paul. God is love, and through Jesus' death and resurrection we are forgiven and restored to a loving and eternal relationship with our Father in heaven. The other is an experience of the risen Christ in our midst. The gospel of the kingdom — which is based on the life, death, and resurrection of Jesus — shows us how to live after we have discovered Jesus as the leader in his kingdom. In other words, the kingdom is about the practical application of our new relationship with God in everyday life.

The focus of the church on one aspect of the gospel (the theoretical teaching) and the neglect of the other (the practical application) is a primary reason, I believe, for the decline of the church in a world that desperately needs to see true Christianity in action. The partial gospel of personal salvation alone can turn into a selfish concern for our own spiritual survival. But the whole gospel calls for a renewed people to become God's willing agents for change in a divided and suffering world, and to demonstrate the values of the kingdom in a just, loving, and compassionate community. The goal is the transformation of the world into the peaceable kingdom for which Jesus asked his followers to pray and work.

Here is the vital question for the church today. Does Paul's message of personal salvation appeal to people about to enter the next millennium? Would a different approach or challenge be more effective? The message of the kingdom of God — an invitation to human transformation — is the way forward for the church and an effective form of evangelism for our time.

A Personal Story

For me, the discovery of Jesus' kingdom was both like the pearl of great price and the growing seed. The kingdom was of great value because it was what a young, cynical, undergraduate needed in order to continue on the journey of faith. If Christianity was offering only what the church was presenting, I didn't want to have anything to do with it. But if Jesus was offering a whole new way of living and a new look at his world, I would willingly have sold everything that I had to purchase that field. As it turned out, I did, because nothing is worth living more than living for Jesus' kingdom. Nothing else really matters. Living the kingdom is Jesus' offer to us.

But distractions, false preoccupations, and concerns began to choke the growing seed. In my life, the seed of the kingdom, although never entirely forgotten, was in grave danger of deteriorating from dormancy to rot. If it had not been for Jesus' fresh speaking of the kingdom through faithful friends and communities, the seed might have died.

By the miracle of grace and growth, the call to pursue the kingdom again came into the midst of my ministry as a parish priest, precisely when I didn't know what to do next. All I knew was that I was excited about Jesus and his message. All that the group of people around me (as a kind of house church) knew was that they were willing to try out the message.

By working through the kingdom meditation course, *A Place Apart*, we opened up the possibility of doing something completely new in our parish. We planned a series of non-traditional intergenerational, three-hour worship and Christian community experiences, not in the church building. We included a meal, skits, new music, prayers, and lots of parables about the kingdom.

What happened as a result? New families found a place in our Christian community. Children felt valued. Some came to be with us who had never darkened the door of the church before. The kingdom brought together, in a new way, the rich and poor, the traditional and the counter-cultural, the addicted and the "upstanding citizen." And interestingly, as I now recall, it brought some resolution to long-standing tensions that exist in a rural community, but it also brought other conflicts to a crisis point.

Jesus' kingdom is great news, but it will not leave you the same. It will demand both joyful and painful growth.

Stephen Drakeford

For Individual Reflection or Group Discussion — Chapter 2

1. Does Jesus' vision of the kingdom represent a spiritual paradigm shift for the church today? What criteria would Jesus use as the basis for membership in his kingdom? (For a Bible study on this question, see Matthew 7:13–29 and Mark 10:17–31.)

2. What are some advantages and disadvantages that result from the New Testament church community becoming an institution? (List on newsprint some of the major characteristics of the church today, and contrast them with Jesus' teachings about the kingdom way of life.)

3. How would you describe the difference between the church and the kingdom? What is the intended relationship between the two?

4. What do you identify to be some of the ongoing remnants of Christendom in our time? How would you apply Jesus' approach to leadership to bring these situations into the realm of his kingdom?

5. As you consider the prayers, hymns, and statements of belief used in your church, do you think there is enough emphasis on Jesus' teaching of the kingdom of God? (For example, what percentage of the hymns used by your congregation actually focus on the kingdom as a present reality? What are the implications for the life and teaching of the church? How could the balance be restored?)

6. Do you think that the invitation to serve in Christ's kingdom would be an effective form of evangelism for our time? If so, what form of outreach or mission could your congregation develop?

Section B
Seeking the Vision

Chapter 3

Loving Relationship

> A new command I give you: Love one another. As I have loved you, so you must love one another. By this all men will know that you are my disciples (John 13:34).

In their daily life and work, the citizens of the kingdom of God strive to realize its values. We have seen that the core values of the kingdom of God, as proclaimed and exemplified by Jesus, are loving relationship and responsible stewardship. Love, of course, is primary.

Loving God, Others, and Ourselves

The word *love* has many meanings in our society — some exalted, others debased. Since it is the cornerstone of the kingdom lifestyle, we must clarify what Jesus meant by love. He describes true love in his summary of the law, "'Love the Lord your God with all your heart and with all your soul and with all your mind.' This is the first and greatest commandment. And the second is like it: 'Love your neighbour as yourself.' All the Law and the Prophets hang on these two commandments" (Matthew 22:37–40).

In Jesus' teaching, love of God and love of people are inseparably linked. These two loves constitute the foundation of life in the kingdom. Although they work together, they are also distinct. The love of God has priority and requires total response. It is not just a warm feeling subject to our emotions, but an act of will involving our whole being — heart and soul, mind and body. Love in the kingdom results from willingness to put God at the centre of our lives.

Jesus sees the love between people in terms of action, rather than words or feelings. Our love of neighbour is proof of our love of God. We love God only as much as we love our neighbour, and our neighbour is anyone who needs us — anytime or anywhere. To illustrate the principle of neighbourly love, Jesus told the parable of the good Samaritan who, in spite of possible risk to himself, had compassion for the wounded stranger (Luke 10:29–37).

St. Paul sums up the meaning of love in his letter to the Corinthians, where he proclaims that — no matter how great our gifts and acts of faith may be — if we do not love, we are nothing.

> Love is patient, love is kind. It does not envy, nor boast, is not proud, nor rude, it is not self-seeking, nor easily angered, it keeps no record of wrongs. Love does not delight in evil but rejoices in the truth. It always protects ... always trusts ... always hopes ... always perseveres. Love never fails. It is, in fact, the one thing that still stands when all else has fallen.... In this life we have three great lasting qualities: faith, hope, and love. But the greatest of these is love" (1 Corinthians 13:4–13, NIV and J.B. Phillips).

The fact that we are to love others as ourselves is profoundly important. It means, first of all, that we are to love ourselves. Christianity has produced much stress and guilt by teaching people to regard themselves as "miserable sinners." But Jesus said, "The kingdom of God is within you" (Luke 17:21). If we can learn this truth, and grow to love and accept ourselves in spite of our shortcomings, we will be able to love others. When we are at peace with our own life, we can attend to our neighbour. Then we can live not only for ourselves but for others. Such love is a matter of choice — it cannot be coerced. When our heart and mind is with God, we will choose to act toward others, and ourselves, with love.

Dr. Scott Peck, author of *The Road Less Travelled*, defines mature love as "the will to extend oneself for the purpose of nurturing one's own or another's spiritual growth" (p. 81). In other words, such love is the result of a conscious decision. Everyday feelings come and go spontaneously, but spiritual love is intentional. We must choose to help others grow spiritually. This kind of love is a great adventure. It also involves risk. It requires setting aside some of our own concerns and paying attention to others — really listening to others, really responding to them.

Jesus is the Model

Jesus said, "As I have loved you, so you must love one another." This kind of love is very special. It keeps on loving even when a person's failings and weaknesses are known. God loves us for ourselves, not because of what we can give to, or do for, God. The essence of unselfish love lies in helping others grow to their full potential, setting them free to be themselves, not being possessive or demanding.

There is a time for closeness and a time for distance. As soon as a loving relationship begins to move from trust to dependency, it is in danger of falling into an exploitative relationship. Coercive business hierarchies and distorted religious cults take advantage of vulnerable and dependent people, and encourage the development of abusive relationships. Some cult leaders and corporate bosses do not want members or employees who can think for themselves and grow in their own way.

In reaction against the social injustice of his time, Jesus identified with the poor and powerless. As we have seen, he viewed relationships between people as a level playing field, and all systems of power and control as evil. He strove to change the system not by the worldly method of top-down authority, but through solidarity with those on the bottom. He knew that the benefits of the trickle-down method most often get diverted to those in control. Jesus felt an overwhelming compassion for those at the bottom of the system — the poor and the sick, the unemployed and the dispossessed, the women and the children (the word compassion means "suffering with" another). The kingdom is for those who "don't count."

Even the disciples had difficulty understanding Jesus' vision. They asked him, "Who is the greatest in the kingdom of heaven?" In response Jesus called a little child and had him stand among them. Then he said, "I tell you the truth, unless you change and become like little children, you will never enter the kingdom of heaven.... Whoever welcomes a little child like this in my name welcomes me" (Matthew 18:3, 5). And so the "bottom-up revolution" begins — the blind see, the lepers are cleansed, the hungry are fed, sins are forgiven, the oppressed go free.

Jesus wants all people to experience life fully and abundantly. "When he saw the crowds, he had compassion on them, because they were harassed and helpless, like sheep without a shepherd" (Matthew 9:36). Jesus was deeply involved in the problems of his time, which are also the problems of our time. He cares equally for those at the bottom and those at the top, but he wants everyone to let go of false values and become real people. God values people for their humanity, not their status.

Human Solidarity

The good Samaritan set aside his own concerns and even risked his life to help a stranger in need. If we in our day are to achieve such neighbourliness, such human solidarity, a total renewal of our society will be required.

But human solidarity can be both strengthening and restricting. Over the past few centuries, Western individualism has led to the formation of like-minded groupings around nationality, language, generation, social class, and religious denomination. Because such groupings support the values and interests of their members, they are by nature limiting. But

God's kingdom includes all. While the kingdom of the world fosters exclusive solidarity of particular groups, the kingdom of God proclaims inclusive solidarity of the human race. Jesus said, "You have heard that it was said: 'Love your neighbour [your community] and hate your enemy [the others].' But I tell you: Love your enemies" (Matthew 5:43–44).

Jesus' call to love all people extends to those who tend to limit human solidarity to their own religious denomination. We may feel a natural affinity with our brothers and sisters in Christ, but our experience of Christian community can lead to exclusivism — and even antagonism — toward people of other religions, denominations, and churches. Being "in Christ" means to live in solidarity with all human kind. St. Paul wrote to the Greek Christians in Thessalonica, "May the Lord make your love increase and overflow for each other and for everyone else, just as ours does for you" (1 Thessalonians 3:12).

To successfully model human solidarity, the church must challenge its tendency to proclaim an exclusive message that can foster intolerance and discrimination against those who hold different views. Through listening and dialogue, the church can promote mutual understanding and respect toward the people and beliefs of other faiths. This task is already a concern of theologians like Hans Küng, who in 1990 published *Global Responsibility: In Search of a New World Ethic*. He reasons that our society does not need a uniform religion or ideology, but rather some binding norms, values, ideals, and goals. Similarly, in his book *Mansions of the Spirit: The Gospel in a Multi-Faith World*, Michael Ingham, a bishop in the Anglican Church of Canada, proposes "grounded openness" — commitment to one's own faith and respect for the faith of others — as a constructive way forward.

An Influence for Peace

All religious communities are struggling to come to terms with the tensions of a post-modern pluralistic world. The future peace of the world will depend on the ability of religious people to live together in mutual understanding and respect. I believe that most people of the major world religions hold many core values in common. By searching to discover and affirm such shared values, the world religions could find a basis for cooperation in building a more just and peaceful world.

In his column in the *Toronto Star* titled, "The Modernization of Islam in Malaysia," Richard Gwyn quoted an Islamic scholar as saying, "Islam does not reject modernization so long as it is aimed at improving the life of mankind." An Islamic political leader also said, "Muslims must accept the reality of a pluralistic world ... and embrace differences and diversity within a broad framework of shared universal values" (*Toronto Star*, 25 March 1994). By working on a basis of common values rather than differing theologies, people could learn to turn hatred and bloodshed into acceptance and cooperation.

A grim contradiction to the search for human solidarity is the indoctrination of soldiers in preparation for war. Military training instills exclusiveness at the expense of inclusiveness. It destroys any sense of compassion by demonizing the enemy — calling them non-human names — to the point where the seared conscience finds it acceptable to kill people with a sense of justification. In our own time we witness Serbs and Croats, Tutsis and Hutus, Catholics and Protestants killing former neighbours in cold blood. Hatred dehumanizes both the killers and the killed. There can never be global peace until the values of the kingdom of God replace the values of the forces of evil in the world.

The Power of Evil

The vision of the kingdom of God involves a recognition of the power of evil. Evil blocks the growth of the kingdom, both in the lives of individuals and in the functions of society. But what is the source of evil and how do we deal with it?

St. Paul, in an effort to explain the spiritual battle he experienced as he preached the gospel in a hostile world, perceived exterior forces arraigned against us. "Our struggle is not against flesh and blood, but against the rulers, against the authorities, against of the powers of this dark world and against the spiritual forces of evil in the heavenly realms" (Ephesians 6:12). Paul understood spiritual and material reality as separate modes of existence. The powers of evil dwelt in the spiritual world and waged war on humanity in the material world.

Until recently, it was thought that the Western materialistic world view was incompatible with a spiritual world view, that matter and spirit were different and distinct. But today, scientists have discovered that the "final building block of matter, the atom, has an interiority also, and that the electrons and protons they had once thought so substantial are not best described as matter but as energy-events ... spirit matter. It appears that everything, from photons to sub atomic particles to corporations to empires, has both an outer and an inner aspect" (*Engaging the Powers*, p. 6).

As Westerners, we are in the process of shifting from a world view that separates the spiritual from the material, to a more integrated or "systems" view, which understands all reality as being interconnected and interdependent. Biblical fundamentalists may still regard evil powers as demons in the sky, and scientific materialists may still deny the existence of a spiritual world. Walter Wink has written extensively on the nature of structural evil in the light of biblical evidence. He believes that the "principalities and powers" of the biblical world were in fact real, and that writers of scripture were describing the "negative spirituality" inhabiting the political, economic, and cultural institutions of their day. "Institutions have an actual spiritual ethos, and we neglect this aspect of institutional life at our peril" (*Engaging the Powers*, p. 6).

In our own day, we need to withdraw our projections from exterior "demons" and recognize the spiritual forces within ourselves and our institutions. We need to become aware of the destructive realities undermining our personal and institutional life. Dysfunctional individuals, families, and organizations may result from a diseased spiritual condition. Such disease can only be cured by a holistic approach, which understands each person and institution as an inter-related system that needs to be re-integrated to achieve wholeness and health.

Jesus' life and teaching made a clear connection between healing and the power of the kingdom of God. "Jesus went throughout Galilee, teaching in their synagogues, preaching the good news of the kingdom, and healing every disease and sickness among the people" (Matthew 4:23). When Jesus sent his disciples out on a preaching mission, his instructions were to "Heal the sick ... and tell them, 'The kingdom of God is near you....' The seventy-two [disciples] returned with joy and said, 'Lord, even the demons submit to us in your name'" (Luke 10:9,17). When the church again manifests this kind of faith in action, the power of the kingdom will be evident among us.

The Power of Prayer and Forgiveness

Evil has a seductive power. There is always a danger that, in our zeal to deal with evil, we may become evil ourselves. The church fell into this trap during the inquisition. The cure can indeed be worse than the disease. Walter Wink sees the tendency to succumb to evil as the root of our problem today. He asks, "How can we oppose evil without creating new evils and being made evil ourselves?"

Prayer combats the powers of evil and links us irrevocably with the spiritual forces of good. Prayer is an act of faith. Through prayer we communicate with the unseen God. Those who practise the discipline of prayer come to know more surely, day by day, that they are in contact with the Spirit and in touch with the power of God. Many find it hard to break out of a dependence on set prayers and pious language. But prayer is not so much in the words as in the attitude. To find God, we need only to turn our hearts and minds toward God. The kingdom is not an intellectual concept but a way of life in communion with God. Michael Quoist regards prayer as growing out of an awareness of God's presence in all of life.

If we knew how to listen to God, if we knew how to look around us, our whole life would become prayer....

If we knew how to listen to God, we would hear him speaking to us. For God does speak. He speaks in his Gospels. He speaks through life — that new gospel to which we ourselves add a page each day....

If we knew how to look at life through God's eyes, we would see it as innumerable tokens of the love of the creator seeking the love of his creatures. The Father has put us into the world, not to walk through it with lowered eyes, but to search for him through things, events, people. Everything must reveal God to us (*Prayers by Michael Quoist*, pp. 29, 1, 17).

Prayer leads to forgiveness. To give and receive forgiveness is the key to loving relationship in the kingdom. It is the only way to interrupt the cycle of violence and vengeance destroying so many lives in the world today. "Get rid of all bitterness, rage and anger, brawling and slander, along with every form of malice. Be kind and compassionate to one another, forgiving each other, just as in Christ God forgave you" (Ephesians 4:31–32).

These words remind me of an incident in Haiti shown on the CNN TV network news. The first clip showed an interview with a shopkeeper who was being harassed by the Haitian militia, because he was a supporter of the exiled President Aristide. The shopkeeper refused to be intimidated by the threats, saying that he was prepared to die rather than run away. The next TV clip a few days later showed him lying dead in the street in a pool of blood.

As one recoiled from the sight of this brutal murder, the camera turned to the wife of the dead man as she said, "I cannot forget what they have done to my husband, but I have already forgiven them." Only that kind of spirit can break the cycle of hatred and death, which often lasts for generations. "For if you forgive men when they sin against you, your heavenly Father will also forgive you. But if you do not forgive men their sins, your Father will not forgive your sins" (Matthew 6:14–15).

A Personal Story

Once I was in Vienna after a two-week illness in a little Austrian village. I had spent most of my travel money on medicine and doctors and used my last bit to take a train to Vienna. I had no clue where I could find my friends who had been waiting for me earlier. I was lost and hungry and depressed.

As I was standing in one of the streetcar stations in central Vienna, tired, discouraged, and trying to figure out what to do, a little old wrinkled woman (whose job it was to sweep out the station) came over to me and asked if I was hungry. Even before I could answer, she took her lunch from a brown bag and offered me half! I was moved. She not only helped my aching hunger, but lifted my spirit in an unforgettable way.

I have never forgotten her — the warmth of her face, the graciousness of her gift, the youthful sparkle in her eyes. We talked for more than an hour about her life. It had not been easy. She was raised in the country, knowing nothing but hard work on a farm. She had lost her husband and two sons in the resistance to the Nazis. Only her daughter survived. But she was thankful, she said, for many things.

She was at peace with her story. Finally, I asked her why she offered me her lunch. She said simply, "Jesu ist mein Herrn. Gott ist gut" (Jesus is my Lord. God is good). She understood and lived in the story of Jesus in a way that most sophisticated scholars could never do. Her faith touched mine. Who was it, after all, that I met that day in Vienna?

(Lifestory Conversations, p. 9).

For Individual Reflection or Group Discussion — Chapter 3

1. "Love is a key value of the kingdom." How does this statement help you to build a practical picture of life in the kingdom? How does it provide a framework for being more intentional about living as a citizen of the kingdom?

2. To what extent are prestige and status key values in our society? How much weight do they carry in the church? How does this relate to the values of the kingdom? (Suggested Bible study: Luke 14:7–14.)

3. With which groups or organizations do you have a strong sense of solidarity? Do they tend to be inclusive or exclusive? To what extent does your faith lead you to a sense of solidarity with all people?

4. Do you think that the kingdom vision of world renewal could unite the Christian churches and other religions in a common mission of world transformation? How would this impact on the ecumenical movement?

5. To what extent do you think it true that religious strife is at the bottom of much conflict in the world? How could the church and its members help to increase acceptance and respect among people of different faiths?

6. What events or situations recently in the news reflect the power of evil? Does the church recognize and take seriously enough the power of evil that blocks the expansion of the kingdom on earth? What are some of the things that seem to be blocking the kingdom today?

7. Spiritual growth in the kingdom involves learning to develop an awareness of the presence of God in everyday life. Why not set aside some time for spiritual sensitivity training — trying to listen and to see God in the news, in a child, in a tree or a flower, in the face of the poor.

Chapter 4
Responsible Stewardship

> From everyone who has been given much, much will be demanded; and from the one who has been entrusted with much, much more will be asked (Luke 12:48).

Responsible stewardship, along with loving relationship, is a core value in the kingdom of God. In his life and teaching, Jesus proclaimed the values of the good and faithful steward. Responsible stewardship is loving relationship extended to all creation.

Building the House of God

Douglas Hall says that "stewardship is a biblical symbol come of age" (*The Steward*, p. 237). It is a meaningful way of understanding our place on earth.

The concept of stewardship is so comprehensive that it is difficult to find an exact English equivalent for the original Greek. Various English versions of the Bible translate the word *oikonomos* as "steward." Helge Brattgard, a Swedish theologian and an authority on the subject, explains that the word for stewardship is *oikonomia*, which is a combination of the noun *oikos* meaning "house," and the verb *nemein* meaning "to rule or manage." Thus the word suggests the management or administration of the resources of a household according to the will or plan of its owner (*God's Stewards*, p. 32, 41).

The word *oikos* in biblical usage also implies that God builds the house, and that members of God's household form a living fellowship to join in the continuing work of creation. The building up of the household or kingdom of God is a shared responsibility: "[You are] built on the foundation of the apostles and prophets, with Christ Jesus himself as the chief cornerstone" (Ephesians 2:20). Every Christian is expected to participate in the building: "Each one should use whatever gift he has received to serve others, faithfully administering God's grace in its various forms" (1 Peter 4:10), and "each of us should please his neighbour for his good, to build him up" (Romans 15:2).

Over time, the meaning of the Greek word *oikonomia* has been extended from the administration of a household to the management of an entire estate. It has even come to include the administration of the universe by God, the "divine economy." In Christian thought, the divine economy is seen as God's plan of salvation for creation — God's stewardship. This is "the mystery of his will ... which he purposed in Christ, to be put into effect when the times will have reached their fulfillment — to bring all things in heaven and on earth together under one head, even Christ" (Ephesians 1:9–10). This is the final goal or consummation of the kingdom of God.

Stewardship defines the essence of what it means to be a Christian in today's world. It could also help us redefine the mission of the church. Stewardship goes beyond the way we earn, manage, and spend our money, to the way we order our individual and corporate lives. It involves sharing the good news of the kingdom as God's plan for human life. But *oikonomia* is also the root of the words economy and economics. Unfortunately, the church has often adopted this meaning of the word, and has equated stewardship with church fund raising.

There is always a danger that we will try to turn the vision of the kingdom into an ideological blueprint to be forced on the world. History records disastrous examples of religious imperialism. We so easily forget that the kingdom's only weapons are the attraction and persuasion of love, justice, compassion, peace, and joy in a context of humility and service. The biblical concept of the steward reveals a remarkable fact — God has sufficient confidence in his people to trust them to manage God's property. The divine confidence in us is such that God delegates to us a unique authority. We are God's representatives, completely dependent and yet free to use our own initiative. We are expected to manage our life and our world responsibly, knowing that we will finally have to give an account of our stewardship to God.

Christ as the Steward

Christians derive the image of the steward from the person of Christ. The New Testament clearly presents Jesus as God's steward. The whole of God's *oikonomia* or plan of salvation is summed up in him, and his role has been passed to us: "The world or life or death or the present or the future — all are yours, and you are of Christ, and Christ is of God" (1 Corinthians 3:22–23). Douglas Hall reminds us that "we must learn again how to let this unattainable vision of God's righteous reign shape our acting and thinking within this world. 'Thy kingdom come, Thy will be done on earth as it is in heaven.' So long as we are prepared to continue praying that prayer, we are making ourselves responsible for the blessedness, the *shalom*, of this world" (*The Steward*, p. 228).

The authority of the steward derives not from the self but from the master. Jesus described his stewardship relation to the Father when he said, "The words I say to you are not just my own. Rather, it is the Father, living in me, who is doing his work" (John 14:10). This authority now rests on the Christian steward: "As the Father has sent me, I am sending you" (John 20:21). Jesus the steward provides the model for our citizenship in his kingdom. The values of stewardship define what it means to be a member of the kingdom of God.

Appreciation instead of Possessiveness

Jesus lived in order to give to others, leading to his ultimate gift of life on the cross. The secret of having the mind of Christ, and true inner joy, is to be free from the power of possessiveness, so that we are no longer driven by fear to seek security in things. The possessive attitude, so prevalent in our society today, leads to comparison, envy, and dissatisfaction — which is the death of joy. Although Jesus possessed all things in equality with God, he gave them up, made himself nothing, and assumed the nature of a human servant. Because in Christ we have already passed from death to life, we can enter into the paradoxical Christian attitude of one who is "poor, yet making many rich; having nothing, and yet possessing everything" (2 Corinthians 6:10).

Good stewardship requires an attitude of humility and appreciation toward our resources. Consequently, there is no place for pride of intellect or greed of possession in the kingdom. Instead, we recognize that all we are and all we have come from God, and must be shared for the good of all. This is why it is harder for the rich and powerful to live in the kingdom as faithful stewards. Yet the future of the world and its economy will depend largely on the conversion of the wealthy to the values of stewardship, and a resulting just distribution of the world's wealth. This does not mean that such gifted people should embrace poverty. But no one with influence can abdicate the responsibility of stewardship.

Levels of Stewardship

We can identify four possible levels of stewardship, each depending on our relationship with God and creation. The four levels include the stranger, the servant, the friend, and the son or daughter.

The Stranger

At the first level a person is, from his or her own perspective, a stranger to God. The stranger does not recognize the existence of God or, at least, does not acknowledge the sovereignty of God. Yet as a created being, the stranger is a steward, dependent on the creator for existence and, consequently, responsible for the created world. The ethical law of stewardship is as applicable to all people as the physical law of gravity.

The Servant

At the next level, the stranger has been made aware of the existence of God and has been challenged to acknowledge God's sovereignty. The servant is a law-abiding citizen, though not necessarily a Christian, and is motivated by a combination of humanism and enlightened self-interest. Public appeals such as "give to the heart fund, the life saved may be your own" speak to this level of motivation. Servants also contribute to the church, when support of the church is understood as being good for the community.

The Friend

Now we come to an important change in the level of stewardship, exemplified in the relationship of the disciples with Jesus. He said, "I no longer call you servants, because a servant does not know his master's business. Instead, I have called you friends, for everything that I learned from my Father I have made known to you" (John 15:15).

A steward is first a servant, just doing a job. But when a servant assumes a higher level of responsibility, he or she becomes personally committed to the work. So say the essentials of effective management! To function at this level, a person must be familiar with the business plan and be able to manage operations in accordance with the goals of the owners. If we are to be Christian stewards, we must have some involvement with God's plan for creation, so that we can implement the essential values of the kingdom. In this relationship, there is closeness and warmth. Jesus calls us friends, chosen by him as trusted managers of the kingdom and the planet.

The Partner

There is an even higher level. This is the family member, an inheritor of the kingdom. "So you are no longer a slave, but a son; and since you are a son, God has made you also an heir" (Galatians 4:7). At this level, we join in partnership. Sons and daughters have more than a servant's concern, because as heirs they have a share in the parents' business. From this perspective, Christian stewardship is a family affair. We are partners in the business! The kingdom is no longer a remote and awesome concept. God has promised to give us the resources we need to do the job, and he expects us to display the qualities of loving relationship and responsible stewardship.

Characteristics of the Steward

Faithfulness

Faithfulness or trustworthiness is the chief characteristic of the good steward. Stewards are expected to show themselves trustworthy (Luke 12:43, 19:12, Matthew 25:14). The New Testament frequently depicts God as an absentee landlord and the steward as a caretaker in the interim, having at his disposal all of the Lord's resources. The steward is confident in his position because he knows that, although absent in the flesh, the Lord is present in the Spirit. Jesus said, "I tell you the truth: It is for your good that I am going away. Unless I go away, the Counselor [the Holy Spirit] will not come to you; but if I go, I will send him to you" (John 16:7).

The knowledge that God trusts the steward engenders a keen sense of responsibility. However, if the steward, through a lax spiritual life, loses awareness of the presence of the Holy Spirit, he or she may soon forget to be a trustee and begin to act like an owner — with dire consequences. "I tell you the truth, he will put him in charge of all his [the master's] possessions. But suppose the servant says to himself, 'My master is taking a long time in coming,' and then he begins to beat the menservants and maidservants and to eat and drink and get drunk. The master of that servant will come on a day when he does not expect him and at an hour he is not aware of. He will cut him to pieces and assign him a place with the unbelievers" (Luke 12:44-46).

But when the servants carry out their responsibilities faithfully, they receive commendation: "Well done, good and faithful servant! You have been faithful with a few things; I will put you in charge of many things. Come and share your master's happiness!" (Matthew 25:21). The reward is not rest, but increased responsibility and a more intimate relationship with the master, through sharing in the joy of his work.

Wisdom

Wisdom is the second main characteristic of the good steward. King Solomon prayed for wisdom because he realized that, if he had this gift, everything good would follow. He would have the power to recognize the right "ends" and the best "means." He would have great understanding of persons, conditions, and situations, and unusual discernment and discrimination in dealing with them.

Wisdom is a gift of God for which we should pray. The world is full of clever people, but wise leadership is hard to find. In our rapidly changing world, we need the ability to think things through, make wise judgments, and take appropriate action. We need the insight of the Holy Spirit, so that we can remain alert and sensitive to the need and opportunity of the moment, and act responsibly with inspired common sense.

Jesus' story of the ten talents illustrates the kind of wise and creative use of resources that produces dividends for the master in the kingdom, and increases the steward's own possibilities for the further exercise of faithfulness and wisdom (Matthew 25:14). Those who, through lack of faith and fear of insecurity, take no risks and bury their opportunities, become sterile and unavailing to the master. The tragedy of such spiritual timidity is that, under the delusion of avoiding risk by doing nothing, stewards run the greater risk of losing even what they have.

Accountability

The steward must be ready at all times to render an account of his or her stewardship. The master does not demand the same of everyone. But he does insist that we all do what we can. The Bible indicates that we shall be called to account chiefly for what we have not done: "That servant who knows his master's will and does not get ready or does not do what his master wants will be beaten with many blows.... From the one who has been entrusted with much, much more will be asked" (Luke 12:47–48). This teaching on the accountability of the steward should give us pause, because there seems to be a prevalent attitude in the church that, when the chips are down, faith alone is all that matters.

If our gratitude is genuine, we will try to lead a good and holy life, and we will be forgiven if we fall short. But much of the New Testament teaching on the stewardship lifestyle suggests that faith and works are equal sides of the same coin, and you can't have one without the other. In his letter, James makes this point: "What good is it, my brothers, if a man claims to have faith but has no deeds? Can such faith save him? Suppose a brother or sister is without clothes and daily food. If one of you says to him, 'Go, I wish you well; keep warm and well fed,' but does nothing about his physical needs, what good is it? In the same way, faith by itself, if it is not accompanied by action, is dead" (James 2:14–17).

Perhaps this is one of the reasons why the demanding life in the kingdom has not been taken as seriously as it should. The awakening not only of individuals but of whole congregations to their corporate stewardship responsibilities, could provide a new dynamic in the life of the church.

A New World View

"Jesus as the truly human being, represents the humanity that the creator desires of all people. Thus the vocation of all human beings — not just Christians — is to be stewards; it is a human calling" (*The Steward*, p. 47). The whole earth is our responsibility, and its care must ultimately involve the whole human community. A shared vision of the kingdom of God could provide the necessary unifying force, and the concept of stewardship could provide the transforming philosophy. Faithful stewardship requires a new set of ground rules for human behaviour in the world. It also provides the basis for a new way of being Christian.

Through economics and technology, we have the capacity to resolve our problems, but we are faced with an escalating struggle between the world's *eco*-systems and the world's *ego*-systems. This conflict is both a spiritual and an ethical issue. Its resolution will require imagination and courage in our Christian communities and corporate boardrooms — nothing less than a new world view, a different understanding of humanity in relation to nature. We need to turn around, to "repent." We must change from masters to partners, from owners to stewards, from exploitation to cooperation. Such transformation calls for a change of heart, mind, and spirit.

With the demise of the Christendom paradigm and the resulting loss of power and influence, the church is now rethinking its relationship to the world and society. Hopefully we are rediscovering the mission, given to us by our servant king, of being a loving community exercising responsible stewardship. If the church is to respond to its calling, the ecological challenge must be seen as imperative. While charitable giving is a necessary discipline for people in the kingdom, committed and active involvement of Christians in the political process will be necessary to effect the huge changes required. It is a sobering thought to realize that God has entrusted us with the future of the earth.

The major problems facing the world relate to the concept of stewardship. Not only the preservation of the environment and the protection of endangered species, but human poverty and hunger, unemployment and the future of work, commerce in goods and distribution of the world's wealth are all in the hands of the powerful. The battle begins at home. In 1969 Dom

Helder Camara wrote from South America, "Stay home in order to help your rich countries to discover that they too are in need of a cultural revolution which will produce a new hierarchy of values, a new world vision, a global strategy of development, the revolution of mankind" (*The Church and Colonialism*, p. 111).

We do not have to look far to see the poor stewardship and greed that is now causing economic hardship and massive unemployment in Canada and other parts of the world. The fisheries have been fished out, the prairie topsoil has been carried away, the old-growth forests have been clear cut. These ecological calamities display a devastating lack of vision and kingdom values. In a greedy and power-hungry world, the concept of accountability to the creator could introduce a new dynamic to world economics. It could also introduce new life into the worship of the church. As God's stewards we have the power to love and to change the world. Will we accept that vocation?

Reflection

We are each separate and unique, but we are also related to each other. There is great value in our individuality, but individuality only has real meaning within the context of interdependence.

The sun on a bird's wing, a raindrop pulled through the soil to the roots of a plant, and rocks falling unseen, unheard in the mountains, are events which weave tiny momentous changes in the unfolding design.

If you cry, it changes the pattern. I may not know how it alters things for me. I may not ever know you wept or why. But it matters still, for we are connected, you and I. It is the way of all life.

What does all this mean on a practical level? It means that any war will have repercussions the world over. It means that how I respond to those repercussions makes a difference to the present movement toward peace.

It means that the fact that people in our community were taken from their families and sent to residential school years ago alters life here and now for all of us.

It means that the way we harvest our forests has an impact on everyone. It is not idle to say that the destruction of the rain forests has global implications. We impact the environment. We affect one another.

The extinction of a single species will rearrange our future, and many disappear each day. If other species are in danger — so are we. Every living thing is important because it is unique and because it is a part of creation, a part of the whole. Each life is valuable, a distinct individual, a thread in the total fibre.

Connections are threads of existence. One could create an entire warping and weft together to create an open webbing, choosing a large range of colours and textures. The threads could represent the earth, the sky, the water, and everything alive which dances its life out on this planet. The many colours of every earth and animal species, the races of our own human species are indicated within the context of the whole. All mesh to create unity, not one striving is unaffected by another. The weaver doesn't know when beginning how each thread of this woven structure influences the final piece. That it does influence the final piece is inevitable. Within the lattice work of essential connections, all manner of intricate weaving can take place with a whole variety of threads.

It is this moment that we must consider, that we must take up our tools to weave within the weaving.

*Vi Smith (*Bridges in Spirituality, *pp. 182–83)*

For Individual Reflection or Group Discussion — Chapter 4

1. Many of the world's problems can be traced to poor stewardship and the misuse of economic power. The primary kingdom value of responsible stewardship provides the most practical way of being Christian in the world today. How does this insight empower you to function as a change agent for God in the world?

2. What was Jesus' attitude to the poor and powerless? What was his reaction to the injustice of the political system? Does Jesus expect us to react in the same way that he did? (Suggested Bible study — Luke 12:22–34.)

3. Reflect on the growing concentration of economic power in the hands of elites and financial institutions. How is this affecting jobs and employment around the world? How could responsible stewardship of the God-given resources of the earth lead to a just distribution of power and wealth?

4. Which of the four levels of stewardship describes your own relationship to God? Why do you think that the Bible teaches so much about the place of money in our lives, for good or evil?

5. Discuss the concept of "educational economics" in which the sacrificial sharing of our wealth with the poor is the most effective way of reminding ourselves that it all belongs to God, and that the stewardship attitude is the most effective way of guarding against the soul-destroying possessive attitude.

6. How does identifying the two key values of love and stewardship help you to build a practical picture of life in the kingdom here and now? Do they provide a framework for being more intentional about living as a citizen of the kingdom?

Section C
Finding the Vision

Chapter 5

From Church to Kingdom

> To prepare God's people for works of service, so that the body of Christ may be built up until we all reach unity in the faith and in the knowledge of the Son of God and become mature, attaining to the whole measure of the fullness of Christ (Ephesians 4:12–13).

Through the life and teaching of Jesus, we have seen that loving relationship and responsible stewardship are key values in the kingdom of God. But if they are to be lived out on earth, we will need to apply these values in our Christian communities and our daily places of work.

A Vision of the Future

Few if any forces in human affairs are as powerful as a shared vision. Because it reflects the personal vision of each participant, a shared vision can sustain the commitment of many people. It can bind humanity together in a common bond. I believe that when people in any age and place catch a vision of the kingdom of God as Jesus saw it, they will want it with a passion for themselves and all others, because it represents love, joy, peace, and a just sharing of prosperity.

The word vision comes from the Latin *videre*, "to see." It is important to be able to see a vision. The more detailed and visual our image, the more compelling it will be. An immediate and tangible vision helps people to set priorities and goals, and enables them to shape and direct their future. A shared vision is a cooperative picture of the future of an organization.

In my experience of working with congregations to develop a statement of purpose or mission, very few point to the kingdom and its realization as the reason for the existence of the church. Often they want "to know Christ and to make him known in worship and service." This goal could not be more profound. But it could be more immediate, more accessible, if it were capable of being envisioned. Jesus knew this. In his parables, he helped people to picture a better world by building images of the kingdom. He said that the kingdom of heaven is *like* — a mustard seed, a treasure hidden in a field, a pearl of great value. He gave people a vision. Jesus also invites us to picture a better world, to see the kingdom in all aspects of our life.

It has been said that a camel is a horse designed by a committee. The Edsel automobile, manufactured in the 1950s, was composed of ideas and parts from other successful automobiles, but it failed miserably. It was not designed as an integrated whole. Similarly, a pasted together vision will inspire nobody. Extensive consultation within an organization, and opportunity for participation by all its members, are essential ingredients of a shared vision. Unless the vision paints an attractive picture of a truly corporate goal, it will remain dry bones without the vital flesh and blood of human aspiration.

Let us dream for a moment. Let us recall the picture that Jesus paints in the wonderful words of the Beatitudes, and imagine what life would be like if the kingdom of God came on earth. The lowly will possess the kingdom, the mourners will be comforted, the humble will inherit the earth, those who desire righteousness will be satisfied, the merciful will receive mercy, the pure in heart will see God, the peacemakers will become the children of God, and those who are persecuted will receive their reward (Matthew 5: 3–12). In these beautiful and familiar images shines a vision and a way for the future. By looking toward this glorious future, we begin to see our task in the present.

The Church as a Learning Organization

Today the church is only one of many different organizations competing for our interest. How can the Christian church remain alive and grow in this context? If the vision of the kingdom of God is to have a significant influence on shaping the future of the world, the church and church people will need to understand themselves as continual learners.

Learning is much more than absorbing information. Real learning is at the heart of what it means to be human. Through learning we develop our innate capacities and extend our relationships with others and the world around us. A healthy organization is continually asking how it can learn from the past and influence the future. It not only reacts to change but also shapes change in a rapidly changing world. This is the mission of the kingdom. The church needs to learn not only how to adapt to change but how to influence change. It is vital that the church turn from "survival learning" to "regenerative learning," so that we may become cocreators with God.

In our increasingly complex world, we are discovering the interdependence of all things. We can no longer expect one person or group of persons — managers or theologians — to do the learning for other members of an organization. It is no longer feasible to "figure it out at the top" and insist that everyone else follow orders. "The organizations that will truly excel in the future will be the organizations that discover how to tap people's commitment and capacity to learn at all levels in an organization" (*The Fifth Discipline*, p. 4).

But Christian formation involves more than education. The process must begin with vision building and vision sharing. Because forces in support of the status quo can be overwhelming, an organization cannot learn without the impetus of a shared vision that all people truly desire. Vision establishes an overarching goal. It is axiomatic that people learn what they need to know in order to achieve what they want.

If the goal of Christian education is to produce good Anglicans, United Church people, or Roman Catholics, then the unasked question remains, "Why should I want to learn to be a good member of my denomination?" If the answer is any variation of "to keep the tradition going," the decline of Christian education is understandable. But if the answer is "to strengthen my part in the worldwide Christian community, so that we can all together work to change the world for God, according to the vision of the kingdom that Christ has given us," then the power of that vision will enable us to learn the values needed to create a better world. "Vision becomes a living force when people truly believe they can shape their future" (*The Fifth Discipline*, p. 231).

Personal Character

If love and stewardship are the primary values of the kingdom lifestyle, then character is the central quality that is formed by, and lives out, these values. Regardless of our personal characteristics and gifts, it is our underlying character that determines what we do with our lives. The gift of a brilliant mind can be used to enrich the human race or to master-mind a crooked organization. The difference is character.

To visualize the values of Christian character in action, we need only to recall the lives of some of our modern saints, such as Mother Teresa, who founded the Sisters of Charity for the destitute and dying, or John Vanier, who established the L'Arche communities for the mentally handicapped. They exemplified love, compassion, gentleness, hospitality, long suffering, and courage. Martin Luther King developed visionary and courageous leadership. Former President Jimmy Carter has shown humility, integrity, and courage in the pursuit of peace.

There is a remarkable similarity between the core values of classical Greek culture — goodness, truth, and beauty — and the values advocated by St. Paul. He wrote to the Philippians, "Whatever is true ... noble ... right ... pure ... lovely ... admirable.... Whatever you have learned ... put it into practice. And the God of peace will be with you" (Philippians 4:8). In his letter to the Galatians, Paul lists the gifts of the Spirit, the values of "love, joy, peace, patience, kindness, goodness, faithfulness, gentleness and self-control" (Galations 5:22). Commitment to these values could transform the world.

Dishonesty in personal, public, and business life could be drastically reduced, for example, by the simple but profound pursuit of truth. Being committed to the truth is far more powerful than any technique. It begins with a willingness to recognize our own tendency to self-deception. Only the courage to face the truth can set us free.

A Special Kind of Discipline

The formation of Christian character requires discipline. But in the kingdom, discipline does not mean wearing a hair-shirt to subdue the body, or keeping people "in line" as in the army. Kingdom discipline is a process of personal development, a means of acquiring certain skills, developing proficiency through practise — like learning to play an instrument. We need to practise the presence of God in prayer and worship and meditation. Then we will be placing ourselves in a position to perceive the glorious vision, and to experience the kingdom of God in our daily lives.

In a world that promotes greed and self-gratification, Jesus' call to the kingdom discipline of self-denial is liable to fall on deaf ears. Yet Jesus said to his disciples, "If anyone would come after me, he must deny himself and take up his cross and follow me. For whoever wants to save his life will lose it, but whoever loses his life for me will find it" (Matthew 16:24–26). People who attempt to save or hoard the benefits of life for themselves may find, in the end, that they have lost the zest of life.

A young woman who worked in a downtown office came to see me because she was unhappy about her life. She said, "You know, I have a good job and make lots of money that enables me to take expensive holiday trips. But I'm beginning to wonder — what's the point of it all? There must be more to life than this." Like many young adults today, she had a church background and had grown up in a worshipping family, but in the excitement of making her way in the material world, she had drifted away from her spiritual roots. She was beginning to experience the emptiness of a life detached from true reality. As St. Augustine observed, "You, O God, have made us for yourself, and our hearts are restless until they find rest in you." The young woman returned to the discipline of regular worship and rediscovered meaning and purpose in her life.

Corporate Vision

The service of Holy Communion, the offering of the eucharist, may be the most dynamic of all Christian symbols of the kingdom, of living together in community. In this holy meal, the past and present and future come mystically together. When Jesus broke the bread and shared the wine at the last supper, he said, "I will not drink of this fruit of the vine from now on until that day when I drink it anew with you in my Father's kingdom" (Matthew 26:29). We know that Jesus has promised to be with us whenever two or three are gathered in his name, as we are in the celebration of communion. Do we have the spiritual vision to see the king among us now, sharing in the bread broken and the wine poured out?

Here at the altar, the Lord's table, we see his sacrifice for us and we look forward to the heavenly banquet, when we will celebrate together at the end of the age. In the meantime, we are joined by a great cloud of witnesses, the heavenly host of saints. Here the offering of money, a symbol of our daily labour, reminds us that "to work is to pray, and to pray is to work." Here the hungry are fed with the bread of life; here rich and poor alike are equal — all servants of the king. This special form of worship should be a weekly rehearsal of what it means to be a member of God's kingdom, on earth as in heaven.

The kingdom of God is most powerfully experienced in the context of Christian community, where caring relationships are formed and the gifts of the Spirit are given for ministry. There is encouraging evidence that the Holy Spirit is stirring up new life in all branches of the church throughout the world, not only in the spectacular megachurches of Asia and Africa. Palmer Becker has noted this recent development.

> More and more people around the world are going to small groups to satisfy their needs for deeper relationships, a more meaningful spiritual life, and emotional support.... People are looking for more than health and wealth. They are looking for a climate of acceptance, genuineness, and empathy (*Called to Care*, p.16).

The idea of working and worshipping together in small groups is becoming publishable news, as evidenced by an article in a major daily newspaper.

> If you ask anybody what community means, you'll get a confused response. But for people of faith, the concept is experiencing a renaissance, of sorts. Small faith communities—people coming together to share common interests, convictions, and visions — are flourishing" (*Toronto Star*, 15 November 1997).

In recent years, many books have been written about the end of Christendom and the struggle of the church to adapt to the present and prepare for the future. Change is needed. But because traditional religious practices have become so dear to the hearts of many, change is painful. It is my belief that the church will rediscover its true role, and regain strength, when it sees God's purpose as the establishment of the kingdom of God on earth, and the church as a means to that end rather than as an end in itself. Such a refocusing could free the church to relinquish some of its self-made traditions and embrace constructive new forms.

Small-Group Ministry

I believe that small-group ministry and team learning are the most effective means of manifesting and expanding the kingdom.

The fastest growing churches are operating on this model. You may say, "So what's new? Churches have always worked in small groups for study and discussion." Yes, but such groups have tended to be peripheral to the ongoing life of the congregation. What I am advocating is a radical restructuring of the congregation around group ministry. Here the caring and outreach of the church are done by the laity, whose spiritual life is nurtured and developed in small groups, ranging from five to twelve people.

A balanced and effective Christian life requires three modes of participation.

1. Corporate worship of the gathered community, to celebrate together our relationship with God in praise and thanksgiving.
2. Time alone with God in private prayer and devotional life, to nurture personal regeneration and growth.
3. Small-group ministry in the home, to study the scriptures, share insights, pray together, and minister to one another.

Traditionally the first two levels have been considered the basic requirement for a Christian lifestyle. Perhaps they did meet the need in a former time, but not today. The missing link is the third level, the "livingroom fellowship," the small group meeting in a home — with trained and supported lay leadership — where the "relational" experience can take place, where people get to know, understand, and care for each other as brothers and sisters in Christ. As they study scripture, share experiences, and pray together, people develop a sense of mission and purpose beyond themselves, a calling from God to manifest a kingdom that will meet the needs of their community and the world.

The essence of Christian life is community. Without a close-knit caring community, there is no kingdom power. The whole church, the entire body of Christ, can become involved in the mission and ministry of the kingdom — not just the professional clergy, many of whom are experiencing burnout from the demands of the present system. To effect this exciting development, the role of the clergy must change from ministering to a passive laity to equipping and supporting the laity in group ministry.

The human body and its cells provide an analogy for the Christian community. The life of some cells depends on the life of other cells. And the life of the whole body depends upon the life of all the cells. The cells, first among themselves, and then in relation to the entire organism, are interdependent. And so is the body of Christ, the Christian community. Christians cannot survive apart from others in the community. We find our meaning and function in relation to each other and to the body as a whole. And the purpose of all the members of Christ's body is the extension of his kingdom on earth.

St. Paul gives us some practical advice about the different kinds of ministry in the kingdom. These are typical of the ministries now being exercised in small cell groups developing in the church. He wrote, "If you help, just help, don't take over; if you teach, stick to your teaching; if you give encouraging guidance, be careful that you don't get bossy; if you are put in charge, don't manipulate; if you are called to give aid to people in distress, keep your eyes open, and be quick to respond; if you work with the disadvantaged, don't let yourself get irritated with them or depressed by them. Keep a smile on your face" (*The Message*, Romans 12:7–8).

Building Small Groups

In a book that continues to be important for the church in our time, *The Go Between God*, Bishop John Taylor writes,

> The essential unit in which the church exists must be small enough to enable all its members to find one another in mutual awareness, yet large enough for them to be an embodiment of the life of the Kingdom.... It is the "little congregations" [small groups] which must

become normative if the church is to respond to the Spirit's movements in the life of the world.

To treat these smaller units of Christian presence as being truly the local church in all its fullness and responsibility means that we should expect their activities to include as completely as possible four different aspects of Christian life and witness, namely reflection, service, worship and evangelism" (*The Go Between God*, pp. 148–49).

Conscientious *reflection* on the Bible helps to relate biblical insights and values to contemporary needs and concerns. Such reflection is productive when it leads to practical *service*. Small-group *worship* can take many forms, from extemporary prayer and singing to a simple sharing of bread and wine or a more formal communion service. Many groups keep an empty chair in their midst as a constant reminder of their responsibility to *reach out* and invite into the circle the seekers and the uncommitted.

The key to this movement of the Spirit is training and supervision. The role of the pastor or other qualified leader is to enlist and train small-group leaders, and to support group leaders and apprentice leaders in regular meetings. The necessary shift in clerical responsibility can take place only when the life of the congregation is intentionally restructured to make it possible. William Easum, a pastor and seminar leader on church growth through small groups, identifies seven key elements in the life of the early Christian communities of the first century.

1. The primary task was to establish Christian community.
2. The goal was to bring the kingdom of God to individuals.
3. They organized to nurture this new life and equip individuals to bring new life to others.
4. "Jesus is Lord" was their only creed.
5. The Holy Spirit empowered the witness.

6. Prayer kept them focused on the mission.
7. Leadership was based on servanthood, not on holding office.

To restructure present-day congregations for group ministry and mission, William Easum identifies eight important principles.

1. Everything revolves around the small groups.
2. Programs support small groups.
3. Develop ministries around the gifts people bring.
4. Simplify the organizational structure.
5. The pastor is an equipper.
6. The laity are the ministers.
7. The mission is more important than coordination.
8. The staff does the administration. (Presented to a clergy conference in 1994.).

These principles reveal the kind of radical rethinking about ministry, and the kind of restructuring of organizations, that must happen if we are to take group ministry seriously, and if we are to break free of the assumptions behind the Christendom paradigm.

St. Paul captures the spirit of community in small groups in his letter to the Philippians: "If [Christ's] love has made any difference in your life, if being in a community of the Spirit means anything to you, if you have a heart, if you care — then do me a favour: Agree with each other, love each other, be deep-spirited friends. Don't push your way to the front; don't sweet talk your way to the top. Put yourself aside, and help others get ahead. Don't be obsessed with getting your own advantage. Forget yourselves long enough to lend a helping hand" (*The Message*, Philippians 2:1–4).

How different our lives would be if this kind of kingdom philosophy were operative in our society and our world.

A Personal Story

When Jesus talked to people, he most frequently spoke about a way of living that he called "the kingdom of God." The way in which he lived, his actions of healing and teaching, the friends he chose, the people he embraced and ate with, the risks he took, the confrontations that he provoked, and ultimately his death on the cross and his resurrection, demonstrated what it meant to live in this kingdom. He invites us to follow him, to enter and live in the kingdom.

Finding the kingdom is not always easy. As a church leader, I frequently find myself entering and pointing the way toward the kingdom of the church, rather than the place about which Jesus spoke. The kingdom of the church can be a door to the kingdom, but it can also be a *cul-de-sac*. Religion is a dangerous thing, as Jesus and the prophets pointed out, and it can as easily lead us away from truth as into it.

As I seek to live in the kingdom, I find myself challenged to both see life in a new way and to act in a new way. Both are very simple and very hard at the same time. They are simple in that Jesus said children can and do understand and embody the dynamics of the kingdom. The seeing and acting are as simple as seeing and helping a beaten person by the road or as searching diligently for some money that has been lost.

But there is a hardness about this living, too. It is hard, as a mature adult, to grasp that I need to become child-like and to experience the trauma of birth again, birth from above. It is hard to orient my vision to the upsidedownness of the kingdom of God in which the poor are called blessed and happy, where real strength is found when power is relinquished and where the rich are those who have given everything away. It is hard to find the gate and the narrow way. It is hard to step out of the frantic rhythm of competitive life into the slower rhythm of the kingdom.

Jesus is the king, and when we follow him into his kingdom, we find ourselves changed. I have friends I never thought I would have. Betty and Rose who are prostitutes. David and

Sydney who are generous people of dignity and wisdom. They are also street people. I find myself wanting to spend less time in the office and more time with people. I find myself struggling, and succeeding sometimes, to slow down and be more observant of what is going on around me, trying to notice where the doorway into the kingdom is opening up in a conversation, in a chance encounter, in a look of pain. I find myself wanting to sing a new song to the Lord, a song that expresses the fullness of joy and peace, the *shalom* of praise that the king wants for us and for the whole creation. Jesus is alive and the kingdom is now.

Gordon Finney

For Individual Reflection or Group Discussion — Chapter 5

1. If the church is to be a learning organization, is the weekly sermon enough to develop Christian character in the membership? How can we help people to think in kingdom terms and to be more intentional about applying kingdom values in daily life?

2. If character formation and the cultivation of the fruit of the Spirit are the heart of the Christian value formation process, how can we be more intentional about this process in our own lives and in the church?

3. What disciplines do you find most helpful as a way of strengthening your discipleship? Is church membership too easy? How could the church be encouraging a more disciplined lifestyle?

4. Take time to meditate on the form of communion service used in your church. Try seeing it as a model or foretaste of the kingdom on earth. Let it empower you for life in the kingdom in daily communion with the king.

5. Is the development of these "livingroom fellowship" groups a missing link in your congregation? What can we do to foster group ministry in the church? (The book *A Place Apart: Meditations on Living the Kingdom* by Robert King with Adele and Gordon Finney, published by the Anglican Book Centre, provides practical Bible study of Jesus' teaching on the kingdom of God.)

6. How can small groups help us to discover and use our gifts and abilities? The New Testament teaches much about the work of the Holy Spirit and how spiritual gifts are available to empower us to serve in the kingdom. (Suggested Bible study — 1 Corinthians 12:1–31 and Romans 12:3–8.)

7. Reflect on William Easum's list of key elements of Christian community, and the principles involved in developing a group based ministry in a congregation. Consider how these ideas might be applied in your congregation.

Chapter 6
The Kingdom World

> The Church must no longer accept the role of a department of religion in human life (Bishop John V. Taylor).

We have seen that character and self-discipline are the means of living out the kingdom values of love and stewardship, and that the gifts of the Spirit are given to the Christian community to advance Christ's mission in the world. At the heart of this mission is the call to righteousness of life — love and stewardship expressed in ethics and executed with justice.

Righteousness

God created the world to function according to law. The disciplines of science and jurisprudence know this. All of life is inter-related. The physical and biological worlds depend on each other. There is a "grain" to the structure of the universe. To go against the grain is to encounter painful splinters. To go with the grain is to discover life as the creator planned it. This is the systems view of life that we encountered earlier.

After pointing to the basic things that people worry about in life, Jesus revealed the secret of the kingdom of God, the heart of his teaching: "Seek first [God's] kingdom and his righteousness, and all these things will be given to you as well" (Matthew 6:33–34). Aligning our priorities with the way of God can transform life on earth. Right belief is important, but right actions are the essence of living. "Let justice roll on like a river, righteousness like a never-failing stream!" (Amos 5:24).

Right living and justice go beyond merely keeping the law. Jesus looked behind the law to the divine intent. We need to exercise this kind of insight, because we can so easily twist the law to suit our own ends. In our time, the rich can buy the services of the unscrupulous to cheat the law and thwart the cause of justice. This is why Jesus said, "I tell you that unless your righteousness surpasses that of the Pharisees and the teachers of the law, you will certainly not enter the kingdom of heaven" (Matthew 5:20). In his great sermon on the mount, Jesus stated, "Blessed are those who hunger and thirst for righteousness, for they will be filled" (Matthew 5:6).

Our disillusioned world is losing its optimistic belief in inevitable progress. The traditional paradigms are failing us spectacularly. Although spiritual hunger is on the rise, the Christian moral foundations of Western society are in danger of crumbling. Generations of young people are being allowed to grow up without benefit of a tested value system to guide them in the important decisions of life. There is a desperate need for a practical spirituality. The vision of the kingdom — a just society based on love, compassion, and humility — promises a practical world paradigm and a way for the future.

Politics has the potential for being a spiritual process. But today politics seems entirely secular, driven by group interest and personal ambition, by privilege and power. Democracy affirms the equality of all persons before the law. Christianity affirms the dignity and worth of the individual. To find a just balance between the rights of the individual and the rights of the community is the spiritual task of an enlightened political system.

Christian Ethics in the Workplace

Christian ethics is the value system of the kingdom of God. The word *ethics* does not appear in the Bible. But since ethics is about right behaviour, it has the same meaning as the biblical concept of righteousness. Webster defines it as "the science of moral duty, or the science of ideal human character." The kingdom of God is a righteous kingdom, an ethical kingdom, based on ultimate values.

Ethical concerns enter into all areas of our lives — personal, family, church, business, commerce, economics, politics, environment. Ethics provides the rules by which we play the game of life. But in times of rapid and radical change, many of the old rules no longer work, and we are prompted to ask who sets the rules and on what criteria? The responsible management of resources, both human and material, is one of the foundations of ethics in the kingdom of God. Good stewardship is particularly important in bringing accountability to business.

It is important to distinguish between ethics and morality. Although they do not mean the same thing, people tend to use them interchangeably. This leads to a lot of confusion and fuzzy thinking, and reinforces the relativism prevalent in our society. The word morality comes from the Latin word *mores*, which refers to generally accepted behaviour and social custom as expressed in law. Morality is thus a result of social consensus. The word ethics comes from the Greek word *ethos*, which means the moral ideal or the universal principle behind a particular morality. Ethics is therefore based on ultimate values. The ethics of the kingdom embody ultimate values, because they flow from the one who is "the way, the truth, and the life."

In 1979 I had the privilege of helping to found the King-Bay Chaplaincy in the heart of the downtown Toronto business community. During my thirteen years of ministry with the chaplaincy, I noticed a steady growth in the concern for ethics. There were many reasons for this. Sophisticated investigative reporting was uncovering massive corruption, dishonesty, and injustice in business, government, and private life. Hostile takeovers for quick profits had replaced the more challenging practice of creating new enterprises. The philosophy of the Reagan administration had encouraged such personal and corporate greed that North America was experiencing business scandals on a shocking scale.

During a severe recession in the 1980s, the King-Bay Chaplaincy developed an innovative program called Operation

Bootstrap, to help the many business and professional people who were suddenly losing their jobs. It was not a religious program as such, but the leaders demonstrated the values of the kingdom. Within the context of a caring and supportive community, participants reconsidered the values that had been driving their lives in the workplace. Many discovered a new sense of vocation. Some changed careers. Others found a new creativity and began new businesses. Almost all were able to get back to work following the program. In retrospect, I realize that a practical application of the values of the kingdom really works. One executive of a major oil company, who was a victim of corporate downsizing, was greatly helped by our program. He remarked, "That was the finest example of applied Christianity I have ever experienced."

In 1986 I joined in founding the Canadian Centre for Ethics and Corporate Policy. The impetus for establishing this centre arose out of the King-Bay Chaplaincy's concern for "righteousness" or ethics in business. We agreed that

> our mission is to explore and promote the role of ethics in the conduct of organizations, to focus on the ethical dimension of decision-making, and to provide resources for business, government, labour, and other groups in society that are concerned with the ethical issues in management.

Over the years, the centre has hosted seminars on many topics reflecting the stewardship concerns of the kingdom — workplace equality, ethics in the media, ethics in hard times, business and the environment, changing values and their impact on the workplace, developing and maintaining an ethical corporate culture. The work of the centre is now widely known in Canada.

Most of the Fortune 500 companies now have published codes of ethics. Many have full-time ethicists on staff to help introduce ethical norms into corporate culture. This is encouraging progress, but we have a long way to go. In tough economic times, codes of ethics can become mere window dressing. Many business people are forced to cut corners and bend the rules under the pressure of global competition.

The Pressure to Conform

The question is, "Why do good people often make unethical decisions?" Why did the Ford Motor Company decide to keep on producing the Pinto when they knew it was a death trap? Why did the Johns Manville Company keep from the workers a knowledge that the asbestos dust they were breathing was causing cancer? Why did the NASA authorities launch the Challenger space shuttle when two of their engineers warned that it would likely blow up? The list goes on.

A major reason has to do with the fact that, in large organizations, the roles that people play make it easy to avoid personal responsibility. "We don't like to do some things, but it's expected of us." People feel powerless to act outside their prescribed roles. They allow established corporate ground rules to override their personal value systems. Why does this happen so often? I would argue that part of the reason is the failure of the Christian church to impart the vision of the kingdom of God.

Christians are still, at least nominally, the largest majority in the country by census figures. Many managers responsible for unethical decisions may be church-going people who lack relevant ethical teaching and support in their churches. They espouse Christian values on Sunday but, under pressure from the workplace, practise secular values Monday to Friday. If church-going is not about seeking God's kingdom and justice here and now, then it is not doing the job Christ gave it to do. Regaining the kingdom vision is a most urgent necessity for the church. No amount of "renewal techniques" can revive the body if it has lost sight of its reason for being.

During the time that ethics was moving onto the front burner in the business community, the churches were notably silent on most of the major ethical issues to do with economics, unemployment, discrimination, pollution, graft, and conflict of interest. There seemed to be a lack of conviction regarding the stewardship ethic of the kingdom — the need for servant leadership and the values underlying justice and righteousness. Bishop John Taylor put it plainly.

> The church must no longer accept the role of a department of religion in human life. In the light of the Kingdom we are called to proclaim we must question the collective life as well as the private life of people in order to claim for it the future that God intends to give.... We shall miss the relevance of our own gospel again and again until we grasp the fact that the great themes of judgment, repentance, faith, reconciliation and life should be formulated in terms of man's secular experiences and secular relationships (*Christ is the Kingdom*, p. 30).

Personal Mastery

One of the basic disciplines described by Peter Senge is "personal mastery." This is not a matter of dominance, as the word might suggest. It is more a case of seeking to achieve personal excellence by becoming committed to lifelong learning. Such creative discipline describes a relevant approach to Christian formation in the kingdom.

Personal mastery is the discipline of continually clarifying and deepening our personal vision, focusing our energies, developing patience, and seeing reality objectively. It means approaching one's life as a creative work, living life from a proactive as opposed to a reactive viewpoint. It involves clarifying what is important to us, and learning how to generate and sustain a creative tension between our ideal vision and the current reality. This tension can be a source of creative energy for change. People must believe that they can make a difference. But without a compelling vision of the way we would like things to be, an honest appraisal of the present reality can be merely a source of discouragement.

The kingdom of God provides a vision of the kind of world in which we would enjoy living. It can inspire us to function as change agents for God, trying to close the gap between present realities and future possibilities. The danger is that we can become discouraged by our own sense of powerlessness. When we face systemic social problems, such as local poverty and the need for foodbanks, we may feel that all we can do is contribute or volunteer to help. But once we have caught the vision of the kingdom, we can identify with the larger process and pray for the creative wisdom to deal with the roots of the problem.

In the business community there is a growing recognition that, in the long term, good ethics is good business. Those who try to live up to the values and standards of the kingdom in a secular society find that their high ideals may not be accepted by, and cannot be imposed on, a free society. As a result, people who value their integrity more highly than advancement or profit can experience discrimination and suffering. Those who blow the whistle on dishonesty or exploitation, disregard for safety or damage to the environment, often lose their jobs and are stigmatized by industry. This was the case for the two NASA engineers who let it be known that they had warned against launching the shuttle.

As a result of the new interest in business ethics, there has been a significant shift from philosophical discourse to practical application. Ethical analysis and problem solving have brought basic ethics into corporate boardrooms. Ethical concerns are leading to an examination of the ground rules of business, and to a concern for the end result of corporate decisions as they affect all stakeholders, including the rights of minorities and the public.

Christian Responsibility in the Workplace

Whoever shapes the values of society controls the future. Business exercises a dominant influence on our social values. And so it is important for the church to raise the consciousness of Christian business people, regarding the intentional application of kingdom values in the daily management and operation of business.

In the course of my ministry in the business community, I met many groups of men and women who wrestled with the problem of applying Christian values in a practical and appropriate way in their places of work. As a result, we formulated some basic ground rules as managers and workers, and identified the core values that we felt would not only reflect the kingdom perspective, but would improve both creativity and productivity in the workplace. The following are some of the insights and principles that we developed.

Suggested Operating Principles

1. In the face of the many pressures that tend to throw our lives out of balance, we seek to live a balanced life that harmonizes our natural gifts of personality and preferences with the will of God and the needs of the world around us.
2. We recognize that an effective and fulfilled life requires an equal balance of the management or stewardship principles of responsibility, accountability, and authority.
3. We accept the stewardship and servant responsibilities given to us by God, our family, our work, and the world.
4. We acknowledge that we are accountable to God, our family, our company, and our society.
5. We affirm the moral and ethical authority and truth of the values, attitudes, and world view of the kingdom of God as revealed in scripture.

Committed Christians often wonder how to apply their faith in the workplace. The secret lies in learning how to visualize how things could be. How would people relate and function on the job if the kingdom values taught by Jesus were operative in the office or on the shop floor? What difference would it make if our prayer that God's kingdom would come in the workplace as in heaven were realized?

If you visualize it, you increase the odds to make it happen. People must see the kingdom in action to understand it. "For it is precisely in the world of relationships, the world of production, the world of power, that we need salvation and hope" (*Christ is the Kingdom*, p. 29).

Can Christian Values Work in Business?

Many people, both within the church and outside it, hold on to some outdated images of the church and the Christian faith. They retain old mental models. They think that Christianity and Christian values could not possibly work in the hard-nosed world of business. If we have such deeply ingrained assumptions, we probably won't even try to change the system. The discipline of personal mastery helps us to see reality objectively and to work to change it in the light of our kingdom vision.

If Jesus Christ is the way, the truth, and the life, then the attitudes and values he taught should show how the human social system is meant to work, and how management should function in a world that is now badly out of balance ecologically, economically, and politically. Contrary to popular misconceptions, business can be both ethical and successful. Greed may sow the seeds of its own destruction, but businesses that treat people with love, dignity, and respect will prosper in the long run. Many of the world's great corporations, such as I.B.M. and Hewlett-Packard, were originally founded on Christian principles. In a recent address to the Canadian Club, Courtney Pratt, president of Noranda Inc., pointed out the connection between social awareness and business success.

> Social capital is the foundation of economic success in the civil society. I consider it a responsibility of business to take an active role in shaping that society. The broad support for business, the "public trust" that is critical to our ability to operate and compete, is enhanced if business is perceived as having a genuine concern for society. We will, ultimately, "do well by doing good." This is the "bottom line" of social responsibility for business: It's good for business and for shareholders. What sort of

things can business do to create that capital? I believe there are at least three areas of potential focus: employees, the environment, and the community (*Toronto Star*, 5 October 1997).

Our discussion group at the business chaplaincy developed the following eight core values as a Code of Responsibility in the Workplace. These values are not claimed to be definitive, but represent some basic guidelines that can be expanded to cover most aspects of life in the workplace.

Our Code of Responsibility in the Workplace

1. We affirm our responsibility to express our Christian faith by word and action in our place of work. We affirm:
2. The sovereignty of God in all areas of work life. This is what the kingdom of God is about — God's reign in human affairs — love toward people, responsible stewardship toward all else.
3. The principles, standards, and values of the Bible in our business decisions and actions. Spiritual values are essential ingredients for building the future.
4. The value of a balanced approach to all areas of life: family, work, and community.
5. The value of human dignity, treating all people with love, dignity, and respect.
6. The value of community, based on mutual trust, team spirit, and shared decision making.
7. The value of justice, exercising fairness and honesty with employers, fellow workers, customers, and society.
8. The value of servant leadership, sharing responsibility, and decision making at all levels.
9. The value of stewardship, acknowledging our accountability to God, and responsibility to the world in which we live.

These core values can be used as a basis for testing the values and ground rules in any organization. This approach is more fully developed in my book *The Faith-Work Connection: The Practical Application of Christian Values in the Workplace.*

A Personal Story

The awakening of my faith came through the witness of two young fellow engineers. My spiritual journey led me to spend some time in the Iona Community, off the west coast of Scotland, where I caught a vision of Celtic Christianity, a down to earth approach to the faith that appealed to my background in applied science and engineering. This led me to search for a practical expression of applied Christianity, which I found in Jesus' vision of the kingdom of God on earth. The journey continued as I studied theology and was ordained into the ministry of the Anglican Church of Canada.

This concern for a practical application of Christianity resulted in my parish ministry as a "worker priest" in the Aluminum Company town of Kitimat in northern British Columbia, where I worked as an engineer on the project and established a new parish in the community. Here I gained some insight into the *Faith-Work Connection* (the title of a book that resulted from the experience).

Some years later, I had the opportunity to establish a new kind of ministry to the business community in the office towers of downtown Toronto. In the development of the King-Bay Chaplaincy, there was no pattern to follow; so we turned to the Bible for guidance. I have always found that the Bible speaks to the context in which it is studied. Different teachings seem to stand out, depending upon whether the Bible is being studied in a church meeting room, the home, or the workplace. In church, the focus tends to be on personal faith, fellowship, and worship. In a business office, the concern is, "What is God saying about my job and my working relationships?"

In this context we made a startling discovery. The kingdom of God was not only absolutely central to the life and teaching of Jesus, it also provided the vision and framework for the application of Christianity and spiritual values in the workplace.

The kingdom perspective shed light on the concerns of business and industry — ethical economics, relations between labour and management, management of human and material resources, ministering to the unemployed, and responsibility for the environment. Sometimes it is necessary to step outside the framework of the institutional church in order to get a new perspective on Christianity in the world today.

This ministry led me to recognize that Jesus' teaching about the kingdom of God is the key to the applied Christianity I had been searching for. It also came as a shock to realize that the central mission of the life and teaching of Jesus had become a peripheral concern in the thinking, teaching, and acting of the church.

There is now an urgent need to explore the reasons why and how we lost the vision of the kingdom of God as the primary mission and ministry of the church, and the implications of this for the role of the church in the world today. It is just as urgent that we begin the process of rediscovering the kingdom for which we have been praying for two thousand years, not as God's final rescue operation, but as his agenda for the world now.

Graham Tucker

For Individual Reflection or Group Discussion — Chapter 6

1. When we understand "righteousness" in terms of ethics, how does this help us to relate the biblical concept of an ethical God and an ethical kingdom to the unethical behaviour of corporations and individuals?

2. What is the difference between ethics and morality? Why is it helpful to distinguish between them?

3. For the committed Christian, the vision of the kingdom way represents both the personal ideal and the corporate hope, in the light of which we can face the sometimes painful reality of life in our society and the world. Take time to reflect on the things that disturb you about the way our society is developing.

4. Where do you feel the greatest tension between your ideal vision and the reality around you? Try to identify the values you hold that are caught in the middle of the tension. Find some other people who share the same concerns, and pray and consider how you and the church could work for change in these areas.

5. Why do you think "good" people often make unethical decisions? What are some of the pressures we face? To what extent can we expect the ethics of the kingdom to be observed in a secular society?

6. If good ethics is good business in the long term, how can Christian values provide guidelines and standards for effective management in the business world? Discuss how the principles and the business code in this chapter can be used to critique and influence decisions in your workplace.

7. (A useful exercise in exploring future possibilities is to have a group create some possible scenarios of a kingdom based future. Invite them to imagine or visualize what

their workplace or home life might be like if they lived by kingdom values. "What would it be like if...?" This is called "divergent" thinking. It is brainstorming future possibilities. The group is then asked to shift to a critical "convergent" mode in which they examine the underlying assumptions behind the scenarios and mental models. This is a powerful antidote to our usual rearview mirror thinking.)

Epilogue

Celtic Spirituality
An Example of the Kingdom Lifestyle

Countless numbers of people are looking for a new spirituality for our time. In my view, a truly relevant spirituality will involve the way we experience God in everyday life and in creation. For me, the Celtic church, for about four hundred years, came closest to living out Jesus' vision of the kingdom of God. Celtic Christianity was based on orthodox biblical theology. It was not a new or different faith. Its power and relevance to the church in our time lies in its faithful application of the gospel of the kingdom. The kingdom of God is not primarily a theological concept but a way of life lived with a powerful sense of the immanence or presence of God in daily life.

The Celts of Ireland and Scotland were great storytellers who were naturally attracted to Jesus and his parables about the kingdom of God. They developed a spirituality radically different from the spirituality of the church of Rome, and much simpler than the sophisticated and politicized spirituality of the majority of Christendom.

The Celtic bishops and monastic leaders, like Columba, led lives of discipline, simplicity, and humility. Their vision of the kingdom of God embraced all creation. Everything about life was sacred. Unlike our modern Christianity, there was no separation of the spiritual and the material worlds. We are inclined to keep Sunday worship separate from our Monday to Friday lives. The Celts believed that "to work is to pray, and to pray is to work." Imagine how that perspective might influence our business ethics.

The Celts created a way of life that seems in tune with concerns of our own time. We have become increasingly aware of the global ecological crisis and the mutual interdependence of human life and all creation. Roman Catholic and Protestant traditions have been generally indifferent or even hostile to nature. There are notable exceptions, such as Frances of Assisi in the Roman church, but non-Celtic Christendom usually saw nature as an adversary to be overcome, to be exploited and controlled. The Celts saw nature as a friend, and tried to live in harmony with creation. They sought to cooperate with nature, to observe and respect its changing cycles.

St. Aidan, an Irish monk from Iona, developed the great monastery at Lindisfarne off the east coast of Britain. He taught the English people by his holy example. He gave everything away and travelled on foot, stopping to speak to all, rich and poor. He was not awed by the wealthy or powerful. If people did evil, he rebuked them frankly. At the synod of Whitby in AD 664, representatives of the Celtic church came from the north of England to meet representatives of the Roman church from the south of England. They needed to settle some differences. The more powerful Roman church prevailed, and the Celtic influence declined.

In 1938 George MacLeod founded the Iona Community, a company of Christians willing to live by a simple rule, and to work and worship on the island of Iona and rebuild the old abbey. The community has been both a symbol and a resource for spiritual renewal in churches around the world. In the Columbian year 1963, the heads of the Presbyterian, Anglican, and Roman Catholic churches joined in a service of celebration. May the restoration of the kingdom of God as the central mission of the church one day unite all churches in a common vision of the future.

Parables of the Kingdom

Matthew

the Beatitudes (5:3–10)
the sower (13:1–23)*
the weeds (13:24–29)
the mustard seed and yeast (13:31–35)*
the hidden treasure and the pearl (13:44–46)
the net (13:47–52)
who is greatest in the kingdom? (18:1–9)
the lost sheep (18:10–14)
the unmerciful servant (18:23–25)
the workers in the vinyard (20:1–16)
the two sons (21:28–32)
the wedding banquet (22:2–14)
the ten virgins (25:1–13)
the talents (25:14–30)*
the sheep and goats (25:31–46)

Mark

the sower (4:1–20)*
the growing seed (4:26–29)
the mustard seed (4:30–34)*

Luke

the mustard seed and yeast (13:18–21)*
the narrow door (13:22–30)
the great banquet (14:15–24)
the talents (19:11–26)*

*repeated parables

Bibliography

Authority of the Laity, Verna Dozier and Celia Hahn. Washington, D.C.: Alban Institute, 1998.
Called to Care, Palmer Becker. Scottdale: Herald Press, 1993.
Christ is the Kingdom, John V. Taylor. Centennial Lecture. Toronto: Wycliffe College, 1997.
Christianity and World Religions, Hans Küng. New York: Orbis, 1985.
Churching the Unchurched, John Throop. Cincinnati, Ohio: Forward Movement.
Engaging the Powers, Walter Wink. Minneapolis: Fortress, 1992.
Global Responsibility, Hans Küng. New York: Crossroad, 1991.
God's Stewards, Helga Brattgard. Nashville: Augsburg, 1963.
How to Reach Secular People, George Hunter, III. Nashville: Abingdon, 1992.
Jesus Before Christianity, Albert Nolan. Maryknoll, New York: Orbis, 1992.
Kingdom Come, John Wimber. Ann Arbor: Servant Publications, 1988.
Mansions of the Spirit: The Gospel in a Multi-Faith World, Michael Ingham. Toronto: Anglican Book Centre, 1997.
Multinationals and the Peaceable Kingdom, Harry Antonides. Toronto/Vancouver: Clark Irwin, 1978.
On Being a Christian, Hans Küng. New York: Collins, 1974.
Prayers by Michael Quoist, Michael Quoist. New York: Sheed and Ward, 1963.
Servant Leadership, Robert Greenleaf. New York: Paulist, 1976.
Signs of the Kingdom, Paul Bock. Grand Rapids: Eerdmans, 1984.
The Church and Colonialism, Dom Helder Camara. Daville, New Jersey: Dimension, 1969.
The Enduring Revolution, Charles Colson. Washington, D.C.: Templeton Address, The Willberforce Forum Sources, No. 4, 1993.

The Faith-Work Connection, Graham Tucker. Toronto: Anglican Book Centre, 1987.
The Fifth Discipline, Peter Senge. New York, Doubleday, 1990.
The Go Between God, John V. Taylor. London: SCM, 1972.
The Gospel of the Kingdom, George Eldon Ladd. Grand Rapids: Eerdmans, 1959.
The Kingdom of God is a Party, Tony Campolo. Dallas: Word, 1990.
The Message, E. H. Peterson. Colorado Springs, CO: Navipress, 1993.
The Once and Future Church, Loren Mead. Washington, D.C.: Alban Institute, 1991.
The Parables of the Kingdom, C. H. Dodd. Glasgow: Collins, 1961.
The Peaceable Kingdom, Stanly Hauerwas. Notre Dame, Indiana: University of Notre Dame, 1983.
The Positive Kingdom, Colin Urquhart. London: Hodder and Stoughton, 1985.
The Presence of the Kingdom, Jacques Ellul. New York: Seabury, 1967.
The Road Less Travelled, Scott Peck. New York: Simon and Schuster, 1978.
The Secret Kingdom, Pat Robertson. New York: Bantam, 1984.
The Seven Habits of Highly Effective People, Stephen Covey. New York: Simon and Schuster, 1989.
The Steward, Douglas Hall. Grand Rapids, MI: Eerdmans, 1990.
The Transforming Vision, Brian Walsh and Richard Middleton. Downers Grove, Illinois: IVCF Press, 1984.
The Upside Down Kingdom, Donald S. Kraybill. Scottdale: Herald Press, 1978.
Thine is the Kingdom, Paul Marshall. Camelot Press. Southampton, Marshall, Morgan, and Scott, 1984.
Transforming Congregations for the Future, Loren B. Mead. Washington, D.C: Alban Institute, 1994.
Two Worlds in One, James Taylor. Winfield, B.C.: Wood Lake Books, 1985.